To Gloria!
Seek His
greater purposes.

Consider A Greater Purpose

Vashti, Esther and the
Courageous Women
Who Followed

Kalamazoo, Michigan

Consider a Greater Purpose

Vashti, Esther and the Courageous Women Who Followed

"…And who knows but that you have come to your royal position for such a time as this?"

Esther 4:14

Denise L. Posie

Copyright 2015 by Denise L. Posie

All rights reserved. No part of this publication may be reproduced, stored in a retrieval system, or transmitted in any form by any means-electronic, mechanical, photocopy, recording, or any other except for brief quotations in printed reviews, without prior permission of the copyright holder.

Consider a Greater Purpose:
Vashti, Esther and the Courageous Women Who Followed

Published by DLP Ministries (Daily Living with Purpose)
in collaboration with Season Press LLC
Design and layout by
Fortitude Graphic Design and Printing

Unless otherwise noted, all scriptures for this book are taken from:
THE HOLY BIBLE, NEW INTERNATIONAL VERSION®, NIV®
Copyright © 1973, 1978, 1984, 2011 by Biblica, Inc.® Used by permission.
All rights reserved worldwide.

Holy Bible, New Living Translation copyright © 1996, 2004, 2007, 2013 by Tyndale House Foundation. Used by permission of Tyndale House Publishers Inc., Carol Stream, Illinois 60188. All rights reserved. New Living, NLT, and the New Living Translation logo are registered trademarks of Tyndale House Publishers.

1.Queen Esther 2. Queen Vashti 3. Women of the Bible
4. Women in history 5. Spiritual 6. Motivational

Includes bibliographical references

ISBN: 0-974-1611-7-9
ISBN: 978-0-9741611-7-4

Published in the United States

First Edition
1 3 5 7 9 10 8 6 4 2

Dedication

*To my mother,
the late Hettie L. Posie
(June 19, 1927 – November 26, 2010)*

Table of Contents

Acknowledgments .... *xi*

Introduction .... *xiii*

Chapter 1: Rocking the Boat *17*

Chapter 2: The Search is On *35*

Chapter 3: Preparing to Meet the King *47*

Chapter 4: Leaving the Harem *73*

Chapter 5: In the Presence of Royalty *87*

Chapter 6: The Presence of Evil in the Palace *103*

Chapter 7: The Beauty and Strength of Community ... *117*

Chapter 8: Extending the Gold Scepter *151*

Chapter 9: Setting the Stage *163*

Chapter 10: Accomplishing God's Mission *177*

A Letter from Esther to 21st Century Women of Courage ... *192*

Afterword *205*

The Author *209*

Bibliography and Further Reading *212*

Acknowledgments

I am so grateful for the opportunity to write my first book. Many friends and associates encouraged me to keep writing. I took their advice and thank them for prodding me over these seven years to accomplish my dream.

I deeply appreciate the support I received from some wonderful women of God. I thank Cheryl Warren for being on this journey with me. Thank you Norma Daniel-Jones, Mary Starks and the Rev. Yvonne Frederick for much encouragement and prayer support. Thank you Aaron and Jackie Cantrell for allowing me to visit your home over the years to have a professional picture taken and good conversations about leadership.

In preparation for me writing about Esther, I sent personal invitations to twenty-two women in Kalamazoo, Michigan, who graciously participated in the *Listening to God Speak through the Book of Esther* event. These women—of various professions, ages and ethnicities— provided unique insight on Esther as we read the book and discussed its various characters together. These women include (by breakout group):

> ***Esther:*** Carla Adkison-Bradley, Sharon Anderson, Jan Baker, Sonya Bernard-Hollins, Stacey Randolph Ledbetter and Tierra L. Marshall;
>
> ***Mordecai:*** Jackie Cantrell, Maxine Gilling, Angela Taylor Perry, Lynne Smith and Lucinda M. Stinson;
>
> ***Xerxes:*** Chris Beverly, Symone Beverly, Michele Gossman, Meg Jenista, Hazel Tellis and Donna White;
>
> ***Haman:*** Ann Dieleman, Connie Farmer, Christina McGrinson, Donna Neevel and Jeaninne Sytsema.

To Professor Carol M. Bechtel for writing a Biblical commentary of the book of Esther and for taking time to discuss this narrative as we broke bread together.

To Sonya Bernard-Hollins, for her coaching, encouragement, ability and willingness to help my dream of publishing this book become a reality. Her suggestions allowed me to expand my book in a way that I would not have imagined on my own.

To Sean Hollins for his talents and creative imagination in designing a product that is a visual expression of the essence of this book.

To my wonderful sisters, Deborah Triplett and Donna Vassar, who have always faithfully celebrated the milestones in my life with love, enthusiasm and encouragement.

And to the Lord who called me to consider a greater purpose in my own life.

Introduction

Throughout history women have often gone under the radar as we raise our children and sometimes someone else's children. We are wives or maintain a household single handedly. However, while traditional roles led to the stagnation of dreams for some women there are those who overcame the odds and led lives, which now grace our history books. These standout women possess unconventional thinking that led to them making a difference in the world.

They said, "No!" They went against the ordinary. They took a stand. From suffrage leader Susan B. Anthony to civil rights powerhouse Fannie Lou Hammer, these women took a stand for equality and often faced negative repercussions from the masses. But, their efforts were to benefit those who would come behind them.

The characters in the book of Esther are a perfect example of women whose actions changed a nation. The story is not a prescription but a description of God's work behind the scenes. It is more than a love story between a king and a queen.

Upon reading, our natural inclination is to root for Esther, the young Jewish girl who had the Cinderella chance of a lifetime to live a fairytale life as a queen. Who we often overlook in haste to get to the good part, is Queen Vashti. She was queen before Esther after all. And, had it not been for a series of unfortunate, predestined events in Vashti's life, Esther would never have had the opportunity to even try on the "glass slipper" of royalty.

Through the story we understand how God does a mighty work in the lives of individuals and a nation. In my quest to learn more about these women I began to see similarities of these two characters in women who lived thousands of years after our main characters. I see more vividly that God is the same today, yesterday and forever.

But, I couldn't analyze these characters alone. I invited 22 wonderful women of diverse ages and backgrounds to join me in reading the book of Esther. In one evening we met around tables draped with purple, blue or white tablecloths (as mentioned in Esther chapter 1 describing the court of the garden of the king's palace). There were four tables, each representing one of our main characters: Esther, King Xerxes, Mordecai, and Haman. During the first of our two-hour reflection, nine readers took turns reading their designated section aloud and without interruption, commentary or interpretation. We simply listened.

After the reading, each table discussed their character before coming back as a whole group to share their insights. Esther's story revealed more than we ever noticed from our past readings alone, or from what was shared by a pastor in a Sunday sermon! We saw how God took negative events in the book and turned them into ones that would give Him glory. Together we pulled for Esther as she wrestled with doing the right thing to benefit her people, not just herself. We sympathized for Vashti who we felt didn't get a chance to express her true reasons for not coming at the king's request.

Although Vashti and Esther have different stories, both demonstrate the virtues of integrity and courage. What was Queen Vashti thinking before and after her reign? What did Queen Esther learn from Vashti's fall? Why was she in the kingdom "for such a time as this?" Both were phenomenal women in their own right.

Thousands of years later, these women have been followed by others who were willing to bring about change for the good of others. They, too, were brought into position and power "for such a time as this." Shrinking from threatening situations was not an option because they were willing to pay the price; and many times the stakes were extremely high.

We saw how being obedient allows God to reveal Himself to those who walk accordingly. We learned what disobedience brings and how God can turn it around. Just as God was there for Esther, he also knew what would happen to Queen Vashti. We realized that through it all, even in the 21st Century, God is still there for us. Even in our human weaknesses and struggles with our own spiritual life, God guides us as we face tough decisions in everyday living.

Throughout history, we have seen women who have been martyred and others who are spared for one reason or another—both are heroes. Esther became one of the most respected and loved women in the Bible's Old Testament. Her decision to risk her life to save her people has inspired songwriters, playwrights, poets, teachers and preachers. Her ability to remain where God positioned her while advancing a greater plan is admired by both men and women.

It is my prayer that this book, *Consider a Greater Purpose: Vashti, Esther and the Courageous Women Who Followed,* will inspire women to respond in obedience to God's leading to fulfill His greater purpose in their lives. I pray you will learn more about these queens and women throughout history whose paths to greatness came with a cost in their desire to change the status quo to benefit others. For them, we are grateful.

I pray this book will challenge you to become a yielded vessel to God in spite of the circumstances of life that we may never fully understand. Even now, God may be preparing you for something yet to be revealed, "for such a time as this." The question is, "Will you be ready for your assignment?

On the seventh day, when King Xerxes was in high spirits from wine, he commanded the seven eunuchs who served him…to bring before him Queen Vashti, wearing her royal crown, in order to display her beauty to the people and nobles, for she was lovely to look at. But when the attendants delivered the king's command, Queen Vashti refused to come. Then the king became furious and burned with anger.

Esther 1:10-12

"I had been pushed as far as I could stand to be pushed. I had decided that I would have to know once and for all what rights I had as a human being and a citizen."

Rosa Parks

Mother of the Civil Rights Movement

(February 4, 1913 – October 24, 2005)

Chapter 1
Rocking the Boat

The Unthinkable

The "Who's Who" from Persia to Media strolled into the royal palace of King Xerxes. They were laced with the finest threads. Invitations had been extended to his nobles, officials and military leaders in the 127 provinces. The king had successfully planned the ultimate 187-day soiree to display his fine palace and celebrate his kingdom, which extended from Ethiopia to India.

Surrounded by the splendor and beauty of the king's enclosed garden, all kinds of people, rich and poor, far and near, joined in eating and drinking the finest foods and wines. King Xerxes was born into royalty; and royalty knew how to throw a party! He was born with the Hebrew name, Ahasuerus and was the son of Darius the Great. Did I say this is THE party to attend? Roll out the red carpet!

Not only does the king possess power and wealth, he also has a beautiful woman who reigns at his side. Her name is Queen Vashti and he loves to show her off. As his spirits get higher as he partakes in much wine, his scheduled entertainment begins to bore him. He calls for his seven eunuchs to go out on a mission to fetch the queen. He wants to show her off to the other men in the palace—and, oh, and be sure to tell her to wear that beautiful crown.

Well, as the king entertained the men, Queen Vashti was hosting her own party for the women of these noblemen. She would not be bothered with the king's request for her presence. She refused to go with them. She rocked the boat!

Now what? Queen Vashti's response grabs our attention. For some unknown reason, she has decided to refuse his order to appear. She has done something no other queen (has been recorded) to have ever done before. It is like a slap in the king's face before the very people who respect him and know what would happen to them if they refused his orders.

What was Queen Vashti thinking? Maybe she was just caught up in entertaining her guests and didn't want to be a rude hostess and leave her guests for who knows how long. Maybe she resents exposing herself before other men as the king has made her do in the past—no more "dirty dancing!" She is fed up with these banquets where everyone gets drunk and things get out of hand.

Either way, did she think about the risk she was taking? Did it make any difference? What would people think about the king? Doesn't she know what happens to those who refuse him? This is one of the first major surprises in the pages of Esther. It is a pivotal moment. Without it there would be no story.

King Xerxes' expression is disbelief. The nobles, officials and military leaders look at each other and whisper about what had just happened. They couldn't believe Queen Vashti's public disobedience. All eyes are fixed on the king for his response to this unthinkable act of defiance. But, he is so furious and humiliated that he doesn't know how to handle this blatant disrespect.

Vashti's actions were uncommon for a woman, especially one in her position. If we pass over an opportunity to learn from Queen Vashti, this is a mistake. She has something to teach us about the role of integrity and courage.

Her refusal to go to the king could have been a spur-of-the-moment decision or maybe she had a game plan. What better time to protest how she felt about human dignity? She understood what could possibly happen and was willing to accept the consequences. Perhaps this was not the first time Xerxes placed demands on her while he was highly influenced by wine.

Naturally, Vashti expects the eunuchs to come back and demand she follow them, but she is not afraid. As far as she is concerned there is no backing down. She is willing to pay the price for a little R-E-S-P-E-C-T. The time is right for no more drama. While the king is furious and burning on the inside, maybe she is calm, cool and collected.

Modern-day Vashti Experiences

Several women throughout history demonstrate the spirit of Queen Vashti. They, too, went against the grain of the tolerated and expected with integrity and courage to make a bold statement. One of those women was the wife of President Franklin D. Roosevelt. First Lady Eleanor Roosevelt is one of the most influential First Ladies of our country's history. I have always admired her for changing the status quo and understanding the value of human dignity and respect.

In the book, *Leadership the Eleanor Roosevelt Way,* Robin Gerber quotes psychologist and author Howard Gardner regarding Roosevelt. "Because she stood her ground...she ended up enlarging the public's notions of what a woman could achieve on the American political scene."

During one instance in the book, Gerber recalls a meeting attended by the First Lady at the Southern Conference on Human Welfare in Birmingham, Alabama in 1939. She came into that meeting and made a conscious move to sit with the African Americans in their segregated section. After the police approached her in violation of their Jim Crow law, she moved her chair to the center aisle—between the white and colored sections.

Whew! She was a bad lady! She remained true to herself while being an advocate for human dignity and the respect of others regardless of race. Another—among her many—bold and memorable moments occurred that same year when she was informed that famous opera singer Marian Anderson had been invited by Howard University to perform in Washington D.C. Roosevelt had befriended Anderson after the soprano's performance at the White House.

The Howard University-sponsored concert was scheduled to take place in the largest facility in town, Constitution Hall, owned by the Daughters of the American Revolution (DAR). When they discovered the race of Anderson they refused to rent the hall for the concert based on an ordinance, which recognized racial separation in public places. Anderson would perform in front of an integrated audience. Public protests and outbursts regarding this racially-charged decision drew a lot of attention. It caught Roosevelt's attention. As a member of DAR, she was outraged and sent a letter of resignation, which said: "You have set an example which seems to me unfortunate, and I feel obliged to send in to you my resignation. You had an opportunity to lead in an enlightened way and it seems to me that your organization has failed."

Her stance got worldwide attention. She arranged for Anderson to have an even larger stage—the Lincoln Memorial. A cheering crowd of 75,000 attended the concert, which opened with Anderson singing, "God Bless America." What impresses me the most about his story is that Roosevelt did not attend the concert. She felt her presence would take away from Anderson who was the true star of the event.

Sometimes we do the right thing but for the wrong purpose. A "see what I did" attitude gives the wrong message. The Apostle Paul teaches us in Philippians 2:3-4: *"Do nothing out of selfish ambition or vain conceit. Rather, in humility value others above yourselves, not looking to your own interests but each of you to the interests of the others."* Marian Anderson would forever be grateful to Roosevelt for this act of kindness and justice. The First Lady got the attention of the nation and world in making an impact on racial disharmony in our country during that time. Anderson was no bystander; she was an active participant in the civil rights movement to remove racial barriers, even in the classical music community.

Vashti's stance also received kingdom-wide attention. However, unlike Roosevelt, we do not know the entire story. While we don't know the basis of Vashti's protest, we do know that whatever the reason, she had to have known there would be consequences.

Other women in our history know the consequences of standing against the law or status quo in order to sacrifice for a cause. In the 1950s, even after 400 years of slavery, African Americans were still faced with laws meant to keep them in psychological bondage. Through Jim Crow segregation laws,

Rocking the Boat

African Americans may have overcome physical captivity, but they would be subjected to racist mentality that strove to keep them in a second-class state. Unfortunately, this mindset of racial prejudices continues to permeate the race.

One phenomenal woman who made a significant contribution to the human and civil rights movement was Rosa Parks. She was a native of Montgomery, Alabama and was a secretary for the local National Association for the Advancement of Colored People (NAACP). She knew the efforts of fighting for civil rights and would sacrifice herself toward change. One day in 1955, she got her chance. She refused to give up her seat to a white passenger when asked to move to the Colored Section. She knew the consequences of refusing to obey this ordinance of segregation. Others had been jailed and even lynched for such defiance against any white person in the South. But she didn't care. It was the right moment, she was the right person and it was the right reason!

Vashti said, "No," to indignity. We don't know for sure, but maybe she was fed up with women being seen only as objects of men's desires. Parks said, "No," to indignity as well. She had been born in the Jim Crow south and tired of the laws—written and unwritten—which attempted to keep Colored people in a place of subservience.

In her courage on the bus that day, Parks said, "I felt a determination cover my body like a quilt on a winter night." That peace comes from the Lord. Though she had no physical allies with her on the bus, the Lord was her shield and shelter!

As the psalmist says in Psalm 91:9-13 (NIV):
If you say, "The Lord is my refuge," and you make the Most High your dwelling, no harm will overtake you, no disaster will come near your tent. For he will command his angels concerning you to guard you in all your ways; they will lift you up in their hands, so that you will not strike your foot against a stone. You will tread on the lion and the cobra; you will trample the great lion and the serpent.

After more than a year of boycotting the city bus segregation in Montgomery, African Americans won the right to sit wherever they wanted on their town buses. Evil did not prevail. And today, I, as an African-American woman reap the benefits from her bravery. This situation sparked the beginning of a civil rights movement that would set the country in the direction of change that those in the slavery-era could only have dreamed.

The "Coloreds Only" signs have been removed. That bold stand for justice soon led to the feminist movement which fought against the unwritten "For Men Only" rules that barred women from success in business and education. Although some of these past attitudes of racism and sexism still exist, we women now hold positions in such places as the pulpit (I am an example of this), boardrooms, armed forces, space flight and the U.S. Supreme Court. These opportunities all became viable because brave women who were willing to stand against the powers that be rocked the boat until change transformed in their favor.

In 2008, Barack Obama was named our country's 44th President of the United States. He along with his wife, Michelle, and daughters, Malia and Sasha, became the first African American presidential family. Not everybody was prepared for this victory; however, eyes were opened to greater possibilities for minorities in this country. As a result, many children and young adults of all races felt a little more confident in their dreams to obtain goals that once seemed so far out of reach. Many of our forefathers and foremothers lived without having dreams of justice or equal opportunity. Freedom for them would come after physical death and the hope of the resurrection when Jesus Christ returns.

Queen Vashti, First Lady Roosevelt and Parks all stood for dignity and human rights. In their position "for such a time as this," God was bringing forth something greater than any of these women could have ever imagined. Today, we see women of God strong, courageous and willing to stand against opposition. We are on the front lines and embrace our purpose in light of any opposition, spiritual warfare and even death, in order to fulfill God's plan. Knowing that He is responsible for the results, we seek His will and follow His lead. He gives us everything we need. The risk of not having status, material possessions and even a lot of friends is nothing compared to living with courage and integrity. This is not to say that He will not give us these things, but it is not our primary concern. Our names may not ever be published in the newspaper or our faces shown on television. But, we live in the reality of knowing that we will always love God no matter what and that more importantly He will always love us.

Settling in the Boat

On the downside, some women are held captive by what others think about them and even what they think about themselves.

This becomes a barrier in realizing their God-given identity and purpose. Unfortunately, so many fall for the trick of deception by the enemy. We seldom consider who we are in Christ, our true self. We listen to the devil and those negative inner thoughts, which call us subservient, stupid, ugly, or unworthy. We are told that we are mere play toys for men, or something worse. Or maybe we believe we are a b**** and whore, words used so freely by some Hip Hop artists and those who do not know the history behind those derogatory and offensive connotations. We don't realize the powerful impact of words!

Until we come to ourselves and realize our position in Christ, we will not be set free from the bondage of inferiority. We must be born again in order to be free from these negative images and thoughts. We must realize that we will not be liberated from the unwarranted expectations of others if we settle for anything less than our identity in Jesus Christ.

These same thoughts and feelings might even show up years after we've been walking with the Lord. It is then that we must boldly reject them and cast them out of our minds, believing that each day with the Lord will grow sweeter and sweeter. When we realize that, something does change. By the grace of God, the struggle to stay on board the rocking boat is not as great! In the end, you are convinced that it was worth the struggle as you rest in His peace.

Maybe you are struggling with an identity or self-awareness issue right now; someone in the past messed up your mind. But God's grace is sufficient. He will bring you out of the bondage of the world's expectations no matter how long it takes. And because what we experience is not just about us, God will allow your testimony of overcoming, to help someone along the way to find their way in the Lord.

The Fate of Vashti

When the expectations, beliefs and/or values of two parties are not the same, it can cause a problem. Accepted expectations of racism caused a problem on the floor of the Southern Conference of Human Welfare. It caused a problem on that city bus in Alabama…and it caused a problem at King Xerxes' party. In each of these situations, these women experienced an intense moment of conflict and friction caused by "lousy, goosey leadership." While Roosevelt and Parks would be hailed for their bravery, Queen Vashti would face a different fate.

King Xerxes is powerful, extravagant, drunk and demanding. As far as Vashti is concerned, tonight, he is out of control! He feels good when he can exert his power in front of the Persian community. She has a portion of her own prestige but her crown came with a cost. She is the king's property.

So, in our soap opera-type suspense, what happens now? Do the eunuchs instigate, "You want us to take her to the gallows?" Do the heads of state at the palace say, "I KNOW you're not going to take that?" Does the king feel, as kids say, "played and dissed in front of his homies?" He loves Vashti and her feistiness, but this time she's gone too far. What would his father have done? He is too drunk to rationally think of what to do in this unique predicament. Queen Vashti's act was not as black and white as when citizens break the law or high treason is committed. No, this is far worse. The king asks his royal officials if there is a law Vashti has broken. Memucan informs the king that Queen Vashti's refusal is harmful to everybody in the provinces, not just the king.

They feared a riot would break out in disrespect to a king they feel is weak, or the women would use this as a license to disrespect their noble husbands. The king couldn't wait any longer to make a decision on what to do about Vashti's hideous act.

He agrees with Memucan's viewpoint and immediately issues a royal decree stating that Queen Vashti "is never again to enter

---

The Esther reading group response:

We wish he had investigated what was up with the queen, but he didn't.

He listened to others.

We really would like to see a strong rather than a weak king. We put King Xerxes in a category where, the man is the head, but the woman is the neck that turns his head whichever way she pleases. This thought comes from the movie, My Big Fat Greek Wedding.

We observe that the king is fearful and frightened like a scared little boy. In other words, the king doesn't have any backbone.

the presence of King Xerxes." The royal crown would be taken from her and given to someone better than she. This would keep all women in their place so that they would not disrespect their husbands. Queen Vashti's refusal, if not handled properly, could affect the entire kingdom.

In the book, *Esther: An Interpretation, A Bible Commentary for Teaching and Preaching*, Carol Bechtel says Memucan's suggestion to the king is excessive. Does the punishment fit the crime?

A dark cloud hangs over Vashti's head as she is forced to leave the palace. She has a clear conscience that she did the right thing. Queen Vashti's name means *best, the beloved* and *the desired one*. According to people in the king's palace, she left behind the best of everything, even the crown. Similarly, Anna Mae Bullock left her abusive husband, Ike, in the 70's and forfeited the wealth due to her from their hit recordings. She just wanted a clean break from the abuse and the use of her stage name, Tina Turner.

Vashti leaves with nothing of material significance; however, she too, may be satisfied with walking out with her dignity. How many women would have given up all of that? Vashti's demise is the beginning of something new although some may have labeled her a failure.

How many of us have left a prestigious job in exchange for refusing to be seen as a sex object by the boss? How many women have divorced an abusive husband? And how many of us have refused to allow intimidation to prevent us from striving to be our best no matter what?

I would like to believe that Vashti did not live with any guilt or shame. She felt her refusal to succumb to the king's beck-and call that evening, was the right thing to do. And while she didn't know it, it was right "for such a time as this."

Rocking the Boat

Reflections

1. In what areas of your life should you be saying "no" instead of compromising your beliefs, values and faith?

2. Describe a time when you went up against a system (e.g., education, religious, family, government or local law) that exploits or degrades you and/or others.

3. Discuss how you handled a situation where you were misunderstood for doing what you believed was right. What did you notice?

4. How have you helped others find their way out of a bad situation?

5. What do you observe about God, others and yourself in reading this chapter?

Prayer
Father, I refuse the kings in my life who try to use me for their own pleasure. I refuse the kings who do not want me to have what You have ordained for me. I embrace the thoughts of You, my true King. I embrace Your Word. I stand in a difficult position, but I am not alone. I am comforted that You know where I am. Father, I thank You for all the women past, present and future who know how to stand with dignity and hope in all situations. May I know that doing right is never in vain. It is a witness of courage and glory to You. In Jesus name, AMEN!

Notes

Mordecai had a cousin named Hadassah, whom he had brought up because she had neither father nor mother. This young woman, who was also known as Esther, had a lovely figure and was beautiful. Mordecai had taken her as his own daughter when her father and mother died.

Esther 2:7

I stand on the shoulders of countless people, yet there is one extraordinary person who is my life aspiration. That person is my mother, Celina Sotomayor.

Sonia Maria Sotomayor - Associate Justice

Supreme Court of the United States of America
First Latina Supreme Justice in U.S. History

Chapter 2
The Search is On

Consider a Greater Purpose
Vashti, Esther and the Courageous Women who Followed

Looking for a Star

Okay, we hate to see her go, but Queen Vashti is history. Like a new president of a company, the nameplate on the corporate office door changes and the world continues to spin.

Through it all, King Xerxes is alone, sober and no longer angry. As he remembers Vashti he may have had regrets about writing out of the kingdom the most beautiful queen he had ever had. Who could top her looks, her body and her wit?

Even his personal attendants grew tired of his moping. They had to get his spirits up again. The solution—an all-out search for a new, beautiful queen!

Through this search the king would have a great pool of young women to choose from. It was like a new season of Persia's Best, and the royal panel of judges would look for beauty and character to note on their scorecards. The royal social media tweets may have read: "King Xerxes Searches for New Queen!"

The advertisement for girls to come to Susa went viral. Would he be seeking youthfulness, beauty and chastity only? Or, would he seek loyalty and respect? We all still remember what happened to the last queen. The king sent his officials to find his new wife in homes throughout his provinces. They came to Mordecai's house and took his cousin, Hadassah who he had raised as a daughter. She was beautiful enough to have a chance. After short good-byes, she was rushed off to the palace where she would be closed off from any connection to Mordecai or the outside world during the selection period. While she is gone from his side, the door of her heart is open to the Lord. He had raised his cousin ever since her parents died. She loved and respected him and his wisdom. When he told her to refrain from telling anyone in the palace that she was a Jew from the tribe of Benjamin, she obeyed.

As part of God's judgment against his people because of their disobedience, Mordecai and other Jews in Jerusalem had been taken captive along with King Jehoiachin of Judah and King Nebuchadnezzar of Babylon. Mordecai ended up in Susa after the Persians defeated the Babylonians, which ended the 70-year captivity as promised by God. Jews were now scattered in all the Persian provinces while others went back to Jerusalem.

Hadassah, Esther's Hebrew name, means myrtle, like the evergreen. Its leaves, berries and flowers are used to make perfume and seasoning for food. Myrtle symbolizes peace, joy, generosity and justice. Her Gentile name, Esther, means "the star." In Creation, God made the stars on the fourth day. After Jesus was born, the wise men saw the star in the east that led them to the newborn King of the Jews (Matthew 2:2). When they saw the star they were overjoyed and bowed in worship.

When we put Hadassah and Esther together, we have "the star brings peace, joy, generosity and justice." Esther is God's star: a foreigner, poor, intelligent, beautiful young woman created by God. She doesn't have much. Her greatest gift is Mordecai's love. He gave Esther a home and told her of her family history. Through Mordecai's love for her, Esther learned to love God. She has no inkling that she would soon live up to the meanings of her name or to consider a greater purpose for her life.

Mordecai is an example of how God uses parents to shape a child's love for Him, for self and for others. Although it is not always possible, most of us would prefer to be grounded in that love at an early age. The reality today is that many children lack a loving, caring and nurturing upbringing. This may lead to a lack of identity and low self-esteem. Self-esteem is defined as, "Respect for and confident acceptance of oneself as a person created by and useful to God." A life, at any time, can be shaped by our Father who loves, nurtures and wants His children to grow up and reach their God-given potential.

Separation

A courtyard was all that separated Mordecai and Esther. They had never been away from one another for long periods of time since she was a small child. He misses her so. Each day he walks back and forth in the courtyard inquiring from the guards or anyone with insight of the queen candidates. Daily reports about how well Esther is doing kept Mordecai hopeful.

Mordecai's love mirrors our Heavenly Father's love. He loves us in all situations, even when it does not seem like it. Sometimes it seems like God has forgotten us, but it is not His nature to stop loving and caring for his children. Nothing separates us from His love.

On the inside, the young women whisper and wonder, who would be chosen to replace Queen Vashti? Hegai, the king's eunuch, had been given charge over them. However, Esther was comforted by the messages relayed to her that Mordecai inquired daily about her wellbeing.

Isn't it like that with God? While we do not physically see Him, He assures us of His presence in other ways: nature, circumstances, people, songs, His word and witness of the Holy Spirit who lives on the inside of us. We release feelings of strangeness, vulnerability and uncertainty to firmly hold onto His promises of love, care and all things working together for the good of those who love Him.

The scriptures are filled with narratives of real people who survived challenging times while living in strange places. Some of those separations were devastating and hard to cope with. Only the Lord knows the extent of this kind of loss. When we find ourselves in these situations, we must remember our God and He brings us out. He is everywhere. He can be trusted! We will survive the difficult circumstances of life for a greater purpose.

An example of a life that led to a greater purpose is that of The Honorable Sonia Sotomayor. She was raised as a Catholic and describes herself as a spiritual person who does not attend mass or a religious service on a regular basis, but believes in God and the commandments. By no means was her childhood smooth sailing. Her father was an alcoholic and died when Sonia was nine years old. Her mother was not emotionally close to her children, however, she instilled the value of education in them. After the challenge of attending college and going on to study law and serve in the court system, Sotomayor was called for a greater purpose. In May of 2009, she was appointed by President Barack Obama to fill the seat of Justice David Souter on the Supreme Court. The Republican Majority in the U.S. Senate attempted to stall the confirmation, but despite their attempts she was eventually confirmed in August 2009 as the first Latino to hold that position. Her childhood may have been rocky, but God had big plans for her. Today, she credits her mother, Celina, for being a great inspiration. Her hard work in the legal profession paid off! She is a powerful role model for all women, particularly the Latina population, as she continues to reach back and help her people.

While Sotomayor struggled early in life with emotional disconnect from her parents, sometimes an entire community gets disconnected from its roots. This disconnect can have various effects on the people and landscape of a community and its future.

Hurricane Katrina rocked New Orleans and our country in 2005. It was a national tragedy we will never forget. We were devastated by the news that the home of the famous Mardi Gras, the French Quarter and Creole cuisine had been hit by one of the worst hurricanes recorded in the United States. Hundreds of thousands were displaced and called refugees in their own country.

Utter chaos and confusion were seen through the media as images of people floating on pieces of wreckage and being held hostage on the roof of their homes by the devastating rise of water. They waved makeshift flags to catch the attention of rescue boats and helicopters. After losing all of their worldly possessions—and some the loss of a family member—they literally had no place to call home. The heads of states, church leaders and various organizations across the country opened their arms to allow them an opportunity to relocate to another place; start a new life. They were called refugees, but they preferred to be called survivors.

Many of the people rocked by that storm were brought on a plane to Michigan and housed at Fort Custer Army National Guard Base in Battle Creek, Michigan. Their original designation had not been Battle Creek, but their plane was detoured after officials from another state rejected the idea of bringing the survivors into their area.

At the time I was a pastor in Kalamazoo and drove the 25 minutes from my home to Battle Creek to give pastoral care and participate in evening worship services for the survivors. Other volunteers and myself, just wanted to be present and bring some sort of encouragement to a devastated people who didn't know from one moment to the next what would happen to them.

On my first day, I walked up to three women and two men who were talking and sitting around a large picnic table; they were just "chilling out." As I approached them, I prayed for the Lord to open the door for an opportunity to get to know them, their needs—physical and spiritual. After introducing myself, all but one person began to share their personal saga.

One gentleman said of his desire to be rescued, "I was about to give up right before someone came to rescue me off of that hot rooftop."

Can you imagine being almost at the point of giving up? Although I've never experienced anything like Hurricane Katrina, I kept thinking about how God was with them even when it was uncertain whether or not they would survive. I learned that some of them were members of their choirs back in New Orleans. I took the opportunity to shift our attention to the goodness of the Lord even when all of their earthly possessions were lost or left behind and they were separated from family members. In that moment, all of them focused on the One who brought them through.

The beauty of singing is that it transcends even the sufferings and uncertainties in life. Those gospel songs we sang that day took us to higher heights. We boldly sang, *"Praise Him, praise Him. From the raising of the sun unto the going down of the same, He is worthy to be praised."* Church is more than a building.

As we sang several songs about the goodness of the Lord, the light began to shine on their faces. We later brought several of them on a church bus to a special community service in which all gave testimonies about how God kept them. I thank God for that moment because there was no guarantee I would see them on my next visit. I didn't know what was in store for them and neither did they. However, God did.

If He told us everything, we could not handle it. He leads us one step at a time. Life gets foggy and at times it seems as if the fog will never lift. It can be dim like a light about to burn out, or confusing like a map turned upside down. Only God can change the situation or change us when we find ourselves in disoriented places, separated from the familiar. It is at these times when our faith is being tested and strengthened by God without our permission. Being attentive to the Holy Spirit's guide through all the strangeness is critical to our survival.

The Search is On

In 2009, at the White House reception for Justice Sotomayor, the words of President Obama encouraged all people, no matter what circumstances they faced in life. Justice Sotomayor's mother worked hard for her children to reap the benefits. He said, "It's about everyone in this nation facing challenges and struggles in their lives, who hear Justice Sotomayor's story and thinks to themselves, 'if she could overcome so much and go so far, then why can't I?'"

These are some of my favorite scriptures that help me stay focused on who is in control of my life:

Galatians 6:9: *Let us not become weary in doing good, for at the proper time we will reap a harvest if we do not give up.*

Philippians 4:6-7: *Do not be anxious about anything, but in everything, by prayer and petition, with thanksgiving, present your requests to God. And the peace of God, which transcends all understanding, will guard your hearts and your minds in Christ Jesus.*

Isaiah 26:3: *You will keep in perfect peace him whose mind is steadfast, because he trusts in You. Trust in the Lord forever, for the Lord, the Lord is the Rock eternal.*

The Esther reading group response:

Esther had the pressure of Queen Vashti's fate over her.

Reflections

1. How aware are you of God's guidance in your life?

2. At what times do you think or feel separated from God?

3. Recall one specific time when you thought or felt separated from God. How did you respond to it?

4. What symbol, metaphor or image comes to mind when you are reminded that God is in control of your life?

5. After reading this chapter what do you observe about God, others and yourself?

Prayer
Heavenly Father, thank You for sustaining me during times in which my circumstances cause me to be separated from those people or things I am so accustomed to being with. I put my trust in You and You alone. No matter where I go, You are there. I will seek You at all times. Your mighty hand will guide me each step of the way. Though the forces of hell may try to convince me that I am alone, I will cling to Your truth. Even when I don't see, feel or sense Your presence, I will cling to Your truth. In the mighty name of Jesus, I pray. AMEN.

Notes

Before a young woman's turn came to go to King Xerxes, she had to complete twelve months of beauty treatments prescribed for the women, six months with oil of myrrh and six with perfumes and cosmetics.
Esther 2:12

"All great achievements require time."

Maya Angelou

Author and Poet

(April 4, 1928 – May 28, 2014)

Chapter 3
Preparing to Meet the King

Consider a Greater Purpose
Vashti, Esther and the Courageous Women who Followed

Preparation

As Esther goes through the 12-month Xerxe's School of Preparation (not the official title) as required by law to become a queen, even she begins to see how the beauty treatments of oil of myrrh, perfumes and cosmetics have given her skin a new glow. Even those who would not become queen would forever remember the "perks" that measure up to the king's generosity during their days in waiting.

> **I often watch a TV series called Matlock, named for the lead character who is a defense attorney. In one episode, Matlock and his assistant stay at a full-service beauty treatment spa (the scene of their investigation) that cost $2,500 a week. A year of that service would equal $30,000 for the year. That's more than some annual salaries!**

Each candidate in the palace would have one night to prove her worthiness before the king. That one night with the king would be exciting but also frightening. Esther's heart was set on pleasing him. If she didn't, she would be sent to an area where concubines lived with Shaashgaz, the eunuch in charge of the women who would forever hold that status. Unlike royal and First Lady status, a concubine was like property belonging to the king without the royal privileges. Concubines were used for their owner's sexual desires and forbidden to have relations with any other man. She is powerless but protected by her owner.

Preparing to Meet the King

Hegai, the king's eunuch, assigns seven maids to get Esther ready for her debut. He saw something in Esther the king would admire and took her on as his personal mission to make her stand above the rest. One of the greatest gifts to Esther is having Hegai; an example of those who are God-sent to totally be in our corner. Listening and following her coach's instructions were a critical aspect of Esther's success. Hegai shares how to win the king's heart. He tells her everything she needs to know.

She takes to heart Hegai's instructions. She learns new ways of expressing herself and bringing out her best attributes. She is coached with the advice that pleasing the king is more about being than doing. The body treatments and food were wonderful, but Hegai pours into her life to make it richer and better than when she first came to the citadel. Fortunately, she is receptive to his instructions and the two have a mutual trust. There is no one closer to the king than Hegai; it was in Esther's best interest to learn from him.

Preparation is absolutely necessary to get to the next level. For Esther it is opportunity for new possibilities, growth and change—immediate and gradual. Her resume is about to change.

While we are on earth, we are also getting ready to meet the King. In John 15:1-4 Jesus says, *"I am the true vine, and My Father is the gardener. He cuts off every branch in me that bears no fruit, while every branch that does bear fruit He prunes so that it will be even more fruitful...Remain in Me, and I will remain in you. No branch can bear fruit by itself; it must remain in the vine. Neither can you bear fruit unless you remain in me."*

This illustrates one method used in our preparation for the return of our King, Jesus Christ the Son of God. In the meantime we bear fruit here on earth. The Gardener knows what it takes to keep the branch healthy to bear good fruit of the Spirit: love, joy, peace, patience, kindness, goodness, faithfulness, gentleness and self-control. He creates conditions for pruning so that the branch bears more fruit.

> *What evidence in your life shows you are getting ready to meet the King when He returns?*

Pruning can be painful. The Gardener does the action. The branch is the recipient, more fruit bearing, more growth. The branch knows it is nothing unless it remains in the Vine. It cannot bear fruit on its own. The key is to stay in a position of growth. Our hope should be to remain in a position of growth.

Esther is being prepared to bear more fruit; she's being pruned for elevation. She shines above the others. The text is silent; yet we see God at work behind the scenes. In fact, I think most of us can relate to the behind-the-scenes work of God more so than the obvious. He doesn't tell Esther to be strong and courageous or affirm He will go with her. God is silent, but Esther's heart is open to His leading. She remains in a position of growth.

Much like Esther, we don't always receive a word from God about what He's doing in our life, but we trust He is doing something. In the Bible, an entrepreneurial woman named Lydia from the town of Thyatira has her life drastically altered from being a God-fearing woman to a believer in Jesus Christ on the day she met the Apostle Paul by the river. God was preparing Lydia for this encounter without her prior knowledge. Similarly, a young slave girl didn't know God was already preparing her to experience the true freedom that comes only through the power of Jesus Christ.

She had the spirit of divination that made her vulnerable to tell fortunes and was being used by crooked businessmen who became rich by exploiting her "talent." When Paul met her, he delivered her from spirits that allowed corporate vultures to prey on her vulnerability. She was set free, however, those making money from her were upset at Paul's interference in their money making scheme.

Times of preparation aren't always easy, but we must be willing to follow through, because we want God to do what is necessary in our lives. Oftentimes, we get discouraged because preparation might mean "waiting" or "a slower pace!"

Shortly after I purchased my first house, I learned from a professional painter the importance of doing good preparation in order to have an excellent paint job. A significant amount of time is spent in the preparation phase: moving furniture; washing the walls down; removing any nails or hanging brackets; removing light switches, fixtures and electrical plug covers; taping the woodwork and ceilings; spackling every hole; and properly covering the floors and furniture.

It doesn't take much time to brush on or roll paint. What's done before an application of paint is more important. We don't often think about the behind-the-scene work God does in order to get us to our next promotion, assignment, new or deeper relationship. When he finishes the prep work, we're like a beautiful fresh paint job!

Opportunity for Discovery

In those times when I believe God is doing something new in my life, He seems to put the right people in my path to support me on this journey. Sometimes, unconsciously, I wanted to throw in the towel and settle for what I believed I could do on my own instead of working with God in the situation He created for me. It's tempting to take the easier way out or not put your whole heart into the reality of your current situation. These people were a great source of encouragement.

Preparation is an opportunity for discovery. We won't miss our blessings if we allow God to have full reign. Esther's heart is open to what God wants to teach her through Hegai. Some people have problems believing God will bless one of His children through a pagan. He will. I'm a witness and some of you are, too! Hegai is going to help Esther win the king's heart. He is on assignment for God—even if he doesn't know it. That's what faith is about—believing without seeing the fullness of God's purposes. He gives us a nudge or sense of something being right or wrong. Just stay in the moment. He knows the game plan. We don't.

If you think about your own times of preparation you will see the significance of certain people who are close to you. Months or years might go by before you discover God's hand had been on you unbeknownst to those who may not even realize they are a part of God's plan for your life. Might they be considered Hegai-types put in our lives to teach, nurture, inspire, challenge and rebuke if necessary?

They help us discover our true self and God-given talents. He gives us the best person to target a particular area of our life as we discover new possibilities in ourselves. Somewhere I read that God gives us more grace to be ourselves. If you think about this, it is empowering, and a lifelong process.

Ultimate Mentors

Physically, emotionally and spiritually Esther's heart is open in making the necessary adjustments of living in a gated community. It takes time to warm up to all of the fuss— perfume soaks, massages with the finest oils. Oh, so much pressure. In the spirit of making the most out of it, her humble congeniality leads to Hegai's favor. From there, he took it upon himself to set Esther up as the next queen, giving her insider tips on what the king likes and what impresses him the most. Imagine Hegai saying, "Yes, Esther that's it. Keep doing that. The king will be pleased with you."

As Esther awaits her fate, she lives in royalty having everything she could possibly imagine. Even so, during those early days in the harem she prays to the God who knows her better than she knows herself. She stays in the moment, not allowing external influences to cause her to doubt whether or not God was with her. As she trusts God to take care of her she is given favor. Even in a strange place, she is humble, realizing she was not the only one vying for the crown. Little does she know God is positioning her for a greater purpose.

The reality of living in obscurity may have conjured up some "what if" moments for Esther. What if she is chosen to be the new queen? What if she is not chosen? What would happen to Mordecai? What if she has to tell the king about her nationality and family background?

Her imagination runs wild. She thinks about wearing the royal crown and sitting next to the king in their royal attire. Then, it becomes exciting! She and the other virgins begin to talk of what life would be like as a queen. The mystery and curiosity about who will be the next queen make some catty and others silly beyond measure. In the midst of it all, Esther handled herself well.

As Esther prepares for the king, she may be reflecting on how fortunate she was to have Mordecai in her early childhood developmental years. He knew Jewish law and taught her about obeying God's commands. He told stories about her family background, which gave her an identity. Esther was grounded; she knew who she was. Her manners taught by Mordecai were evident as she asked for nothing other than what Hegai suggested. She trusts his judgment just as she trusted her cousin's judgment. She is a good listener and receiver of her mentor's wisdom, knowing he sees something in her that she may not have necessarily seen in herself.

Preparing to Meet the King

It is beautiful to have a mentoring relationship with someone God uses to change your life profoundly whether it is in the workplace, church or community. What if a woman by the name of Mrs. Flowers had not taken interest in a young girl who needed someone to nurture her? We probably would not have read the poems or heard the beautiful, distinguishing voice of the accomplished and admired writer, the late Maya Angelou. In her youth, Maya had a traumatic experience of rape by her mother's boyfriend, Mr. Freeman. That trauma led to Maya refusing to speak to anyone (except her only brother Bailey) for almost a year.

Then came Mrs. Flowers as her "first life line." Mrs. Flowers was a prim and proper woman in a good sense, who wore gloves to set off her outfits. Maya thought a lot of her and later said of her, "She appealed to me because she was like people I had never met personally."

One day Mrs. Flowers stopped in to buy some goods from Maya's family store. Her grandmother was going to send her brother, Bailey to help her carry them home. Instead, she requested that Marguerite (which is Maya's birth name) go along. They left together on the path leading to Mrs. Flowers' house. Along the way she talked to Maya about how well she was doing in school with written work, but her lack of verbal communication could be an issue.

What she said next got Maya thinking. "Now no one is going to make you talk—possibly no one can. But bear in mind, language is man's way of communicating with his fellow man and it is language alone which separates him from the lower animals." With the encouragement of Mrs. Flowers, Maya read a lot of

books, but that wasn't good enough. Mrs. Flowers said, "Words mean more than what is set down on paper. It takes the human voice to infuse them with the shades of deeper meaning."
Mrs. Flowers gave her some books to read aloud. She was told to "try to make a sentence sound in as many different ways as possible." Mrs. Flowers set the bar high for her. Maya took each word spoken by Mrs. Flowers seriously. "Death would be too kind and brief." During one visit to Mrs. Flowers' home she asked Maya to have a seat where there were cookies on a platter. As Maya took "little lady-like bites off the edges," Mrs. Flowers gave her what they later called "my lessons in living." Here are some words she shared:

"Be intolerant of ignorance but understanding of illiteracy."

"That some people, unable to go to school, were more educated and even more intelligent than college professors."

"Listen carefully to what country people called mother wit." It contains *"the collective wisdom of generations."*

Mrs. Flowers dusted off a thick book entitled, *A Tale of Two Cities*. Maya had read it before. When Mrs. Flowers turned to the first page and began to read, it was the first time in Maya's life she heard poetry. Mrs. Flowers sounded as if she were "nearly singing," Angelou later recalled. After finishing the poem, she said, "How do you like that?" Maya knew Mrs. Flowers expected a response from her.

She felt compelled to say, "Yes, ma'am." That wasn't all Mrs. Flowers was expecting of Maya. She gave her the book of poems and told Maya to "memorize one for her." The next visit she would be expected to recite it.

Maya was touched deeply by Mrs. Flowers because she was respected as no one other than Marguerite Johnson. She thought, "I didn't question why Mrs. Flowers had singled me out for attention, nor did it occur to me that Momma might have asked her to give me a little talking to. All I cared about was that she had made tea cookies for *me* and read to *me* from her favorite book. It was enough to prove that she liked *me*."

Another example of the value of a mentoring relationship is told in Dorothy Height's book, *Open Wide the Freedom Gates*, where she shares a story about when she was a young lady working at the Harlem YWCA. Height was assigned to greet and escort First Lady Eleanor Roosevelt during a meeting hosted by the National Council of Negro Women (NCNW) of which Mary McLeod Bethune was president. Height almost missed the unpredictable First Lady who entered through the service door instead of the main entrance.

What happened next surprised Height. As she waited for Roosevelt, Bethune took a personal interest in Height and later appointed her to NCNW's Resolution Committee. Height wrote in her book, "On that fall day the redoubtable Mary McLeod Bethune put her hand on me…"

Bethune founded Bethune-Cookman College in Daytona Beach, Florida, and is the only African American woman in the United States to found a four-year accredited college. Height points out how Bethune believed, "women were the key to change.

Who knew the problems, the pain, and the cost better than they?" She goes on to say that "next to God, we are indebted to women, first for their life itself, and then for making it worth living." Height was a woman of courage, dignity and influence. As Bethune mentored Height, she prepared her to become the fourth president of the NCNW, a position she held for forty-one years.

> *Who has God used to put their hand on you? In whose life is God using you as a guiding hand?*

Height stood with the Rev. Dr. Martin Luther King, Jr. and others on the frontline in the fight for civil rights. She passed away on April 20, 2010. She finished well! I see the image of Mary McLeod Bethune putting her hand on Dorothy Height because she believed women were the key to change. She saw something in Dorothy Height that was unknown to her. A guiding hand was in Height's life—God's hand. He works on our heart in molding us in his image whether we are aware of it or not. He sees the finished product.

Isn't it wonderful to be marked for a particular service? Are you a marked woman? It is so encouraging to know that someone recognizes your strengths and sees your potential. What's even more revealing is that a mentor is willing to take a risk.

In the 2012 Olympics, Gabriel (Gabby) Douglas, a member of the U.S. Gymnastics team, wins the gold for the women's all-around gymnastics. She is also the first American gymnast to win the individual all-around and team gymnastics in the same year. At an early age, her parents saw how easy cartwheels were for her and enrolled Gabby in gymnastic classes. When Gabby was 12 years old, she wanted to leave home to go to Iowa to train with an elite gymnastics coach. Her mother would not allow this, but a couple years later Gabby's wish came true.

She wanted an experienced gymnastics coach to invest in her. It happened. She trained under one of the best gymnastic trainers in the field, Liang Chow. Douglas dreamed of professionally competing and nothing would stop her. Because of her determination, people invested in her. Just as Douglas received the mentor of her dreams, God will bring the Hegai figures into our lives. We must be committed, teachable and have a good attitude.

The grandmother of one of my favorite theologians, Howard Thurman, understood the barriers that kept Daytona, Florida's black children from being properly instructed toward higher education. Grandma Nancy was a former slave who had been denied the privilege of freedom and education. She could not read, but that did not stop Thurman from reading the Bible to her daily.

Through her nurturing spirit she helped Thurman to discover his natural gifts and take seriously the need to be prepared for a formal education. She possessed that "mother wit" oftentimes referred to by previous generations and what Mrs. Flowers told Maya to pay attention to.

Thurman broke those barriers that tried to keep him from excelling. He was a Morehouse College graduate and valedictorian of his class. He studied at Columbia University and graduated from Rochester Theological Seminary. He worked with Bethune and intellectuals at Boston and Howard universities, where he became Dean of Chapel. He went on to write twenty-one books and was the founder of one of the earliest multicultural churches in the United States. In his life we see the fruit of a Negro slave woman! It was beyond what anyone could imagine.

Each one of us must declare to others how God works His good pleasure in us. What we do is contingent on whose we are. God uses others to bring out the best in us. The late Rev. Dr. Frederick G. Sampson was my father in the ministry and was Pastor of Tabernacle Missionary Baptist Church in Detroit. One of his many sermons I admired was titled, "Life's Vital Vision." In that sermon he shared how we must "embrace the thoughts of who God wants us to be." Sometimes we are so busy *doing* and we don't take time to *discover* God's hand at work in molding and shaping us.

I began to think about how we must shift our focus from who others *want* us to be to who God *shapes* us to be. There is a difference. Sometimes it's not always easy to distinguish whose agenda is at hand. Having peace about something plays a major role in helping us to discern what is happening in our lives.

Preparing to Meet the King

God has a place on His agenda for each one of us. *Embracing His purpose* should be your life's discipline just like other disciplines (exercising, learning, good diet, etc.). If someone would write a story about your life, would your family and friends recognize it as your story?

> ***Who is investing in you? How is God preparing you for a greater purpose?***

If someone gave your eulogy and you were privileged to listen in, would you recognize whom he or she was speaking of? If we are not careful, we will get to the end of our life and find out that we did not live our own life but someone else's. Now that's a scary thought!

When I was in seminary, I was one of just a few women in the Master of Divinity, Pastoral Leadership track. I always wanted a mentor. It was quite obvious that there were few mentors for women in ministry. Although there were some godly, capable women working at our seminary, it wasn't likely for a woman in the Pastoral Leadership track to have a mentor. Regardless, God blessed me to have several persons I talked to on a regular basis, including my advisor, the late Rev. Dr. William J. Larkin Jr., and the Rev. Dr. Charles Young. They are Hegai figures.

I've had several Hegai-types in my life including my own mother, who taught me how to trust the Lord for everything. They are priceless! We cannot put a price on what they give because they give so much without a second thought. Perhaps you have some people in your life like this. I remember when I was thirsting to know Jesus Christ and to learn from Him. In addition to attending Bible studies, He placed it on my heart to watch and to learn from several mature women who were leaders in our church. Becoming a better teacher of the Word and a strong woman of God are the results of learning from role models.

They may never know how much they blessed me, and my own plans to follow in many of their spiritual footsteps. They, like you, never know who is watching and learning from you. God's preparation for something unknown in the present is revealed in the future. It's a blessing to know how God can use one person to make an impacting impression on another.

Over the last ten years, God has been connecting me with the right people for discovery and development through circles of trust, consultation and coaching. These experiences are quite informative in helping me to focus on who I am. These support systems are crucial for our personal growth and discovery. God will help us to connect with the right people to greatly impact our life. In fact, sometimes if we are serious and our desire is strong enough, we might even seek them out.

Consider some of the support systems today—family, close friends, co-workers, social media (Facebook, LinkedIn, Twitter, etc.), small groups and affinity groups in churches and other organizations. It is a lot different than how I went about working with a support system ten years ago. Technology plays an important role in connecting us. When used appropriately and with integrity, these support structures provide an effective way for believers *"...to encourage one another and build each other up...* (1 Thessalonians 5:11). *And let us consider how we may spur one another on toward love and good deeds* (Hebrews 10:24). We have access to people all over the world. We might be totally surprised who God connects us with for growth purposes.

A primary role of our parents is to help us discover who we are in childhood. We read in Proverbs 22:6, *Train a child in the way he should go, and when he is old he will not run from it.* Parents are a powerful support system. We tend to forget that sometimes the family system fails, even in biblical times. Examples of parents failing with their children are found through many of our main characters of the Bible. We see a breakdown in respect for God through the sons of the Prophet Eli. We see it with King David and his son Absalom, and with Haman and his sons in the book of Esther.

In many cases, we do our best to raise and support our children knowing that there are no guarantees. God uses schoolteachers, pastors, Sunday school teachers, youth leaders, neighbors, athletic coaches and other persons to provide support systems to influence our character, beliefs, values, skills and passions. This is an on-going, divinely orchestrated process.

In the song, "He saw the Best in Me," sang by Gospel music artist, the Rev. Dr. Marvin L. Sapp, the singer/minister sings of how God sees the best in each of us. Hegai saw the best in Esther. A quote by Michelangelo speaks of the unknown. "Every block of stone has a statue inside it and it is the task of the sculptor to discover it." That's it! God sees the finished work; we experience the chipping away. A mighty, transforming work happens when our hearts are receptive.

Esther was positioned for change to happen in her life. All she had to do is allow it to happen. God positions us for change the same way. When we are in a position to receive everything He wants to deposit in us, from whomever He chooses, we are on the road of limitless discovery. Life is filled with acts of obedience and spiritual acts of worship in offering ourselves to God. There is no greater sacrifice than that of obedience motivated by love.

In Isaiah 64:8 (which is my lifetime scripture) the prophet says, *Yet, O LORD, you are our Father. We are the clay, you are the potter; we are all the work of your hand.* What a beautiful image of God shaping our lives for His purposes. He doesn't make junk. The potter holds the clay in His hands shaping it according to His good pleasure. He does not set the clay aside until it is a vessel fit for service; his hands are always on his child. The image takes form as He moves His hands shaping the clay by smoothing out all the imperfections—and we have many.

Only the potter has an image and purpose in mind for his vessels. I love being in His hands. With all the bullying going on in our schools and verbal abuse in our homes, we do not have to accept what other people say about us out of their own ignorance, jealousy or evilness. We reject the lies of the devil and negative thoughts. The truth is that God has His hands on you!

Preparing to Meet the King

I once participated in a management development program at a major computer company. One day, my second-line manager complimented me on a presentation I had been working on for a major account. But he also gave me recommendations on how it could have been better. I was blown away. I couldn't get over the fact that I had spent late night hours preparing for my presentation, and as far as I was concerned it was a job well done.

That's what I was thinking to myself. But he saw what I could not see and was willing to give valuable advice. I wasn't excited about redoing the presentation until I saw the revised work was much better than the first. Just imagine if I had been upset and unwilling to learn? That could have led to a missed opportunity to discover something new just because I let my flesh get in the way of progress.

We all have rough edges. Esther did too, but Hegai was there to help her. God uses people to "smooth" us out. If we are going to be used as God's instruments, we must get ready for the preparation. He is willing to invest in us. God works out His good in each one of us individually. When we think of this as an investment, we know all the hard work will eventually bring forth something good for His kingdom. Once we are brought into the Light, we should expect His transforming power to work in us.

We gain insights from stories in the Bible about how God shapes individuals with rough edges in bringing forth something good.

Consider a Greater Purpose
Vashti, Esther and the Courageous Women who Followed

WOMAN AT THE WELL: A Samaritan woman of ill repute has an encounter with Jesus at the well in Sychar, a town in Samaria. He didn't have to go the route he did, but he chose to go through Samaria to Galilee. This is not the common route that Jews would take because they didn't want to encounter any Samaritans. They were considered dogs and Jews were often vicious toward them. Jesus was weary, hungry and thirsty. As he approached the well, he had nothing to draw the water.

Soon, a woman comes to the well in the heat of the day to fill her empty jar. She didn't think anyone else would be there, so she was surprised to find Jesus. He asks her to give him a drink and she, somewhat stunned, didn't understand why a Jew would ask a Samaritan for anything.

She had a greater need than she thought: the water from the well and the husbands who belonged to their wives would not satisfy her thirst. She didn't know it, but she was talking to the One who is the Living Water! Her life would never be the same. After talking to Jesus she left the water jar behind in haste of sharing what He had told her in hopes of others coming to know Him. She came to life and had something life-changing to share with others. One encounter with the Messiah transformed her life.

MARY MAGDALENE: One of the disciples of Jesus who was a woman named Mary, had been possessed by seven demons. Before Mary became a follower of Jesus, evil spirits tormented her. Jesus set her free from those demons that kept her bound. She was broken, but became a new woman. In a spirit of gratitude she provided for Jesus during His ministry on earth and was present at the crucifixion. She and another companion were the first to reach His tomb to find His body was not there. Mary wept at the thought that someone had stolen Jesus' body. Then, two angels appeared who announced to her that Jesus had done what He said—He had risen on the third day. When the other women with Mary left the tomb site Mary stayed and was soon approached by a man who she did not recognize. Once he said her name, she immediately knew it was the Risen Savior. What an honor and privilege to be the first one to see and hear Jesus after the resurrection! And He called her name!

A Fresh Look for Esther

Esther has a fresh look. She welcomes new colors, fabrics and styles of clothing that compliment her appearance. Hegai brought fine linen and silk garments especially for her. She appreciates a new hairstyle, facial and body treatments. She is almost ready to meet the king.

Most women would appreciate a fresh look every now and then. Our total look can bring glory to God! He cares about every detail of our life including: diet, exercise, wardrobe and hair. He wants us to be good stewards over everything given to us. We do all things to bring Him glory. Of course, we must keep a balance and not go overboard to the left or to the right.

The king did not see Esther until the twelve-month treatment was completed. This was a once-in-a-lifetime opportunity to present her best. She took it seriously and understood how important appearance was to the king. Everything the king owned, even his wife, made a statement about his power, status and values. He admired beauty!

God cares about the total woman— mind, soul, body and spirit. We have to be careful not to fall into a mindset that God does not care about our total beauty He does, but not as it relates only to the world's standards of beauty. He cares about our Mind (reading intellectual stimulation); Body (exercise, rest and pampering); Soul (reflection and contemplation); and Spirit (be filled with the Spirit).

I met a beautiful elderly woman at the hair salon where I frequent. We talked while sitting under the hair dryer or waiting to sit in the stylist's chair. I admired her beauty, inner and outer. She always had a kind, encouraging word and greetings with a pleasant smile. Bright colors, pastels and flowery prints were her favorites. She had a total look from top to bottom, but in no way was she flashy. She wore colors complementary to her skin tone and hair color.

A few times, when something was weighing on her heart, she shared it with me and I committed it to prayer. Jewel Clomon was a classy woman. God's brilliant, precious jewel shined everywhere she went. The Lord brought her home in December 2012, and I had the pleasure of giving the eulogy. Her sons called me shortly after she passed. When I got to their apartment I walked in the bedroom where she lay dressed in a turquoise top with black embroidery. She looked lovely, as if she greeted me with that same pleasant smile I had come to love; it made me smile.

Look good! Feel good! Do it all for the glory of God!

Preparing to Meet the King

Reflections

1. Who has God placed in your path to help you become the best you? How do you see God working in this relationship?

2. Who else might you seek for further personal growth? What might be some next steps?

3. What does it mean for you to look good and feel good for the glory of God?

4. What areas of your life need tending to if you desire a fresh look? If you took steps toward looking your best what might that look like?

5. Prayerfully, trust the Holy Spirit to guide you in attending to your mind, body, soul and spirit.

Prayer
Father, if there is anything that hinders me from receiving Your ways of shaping my life, please remove it. I will not reject those times when You are preparing me for the known or unknown. I will embrace those people You place in my life to mold and shape me according to Your will. I desire an open heart in times of preparation that please You. You know me better than I know myself and I trust that You have my best interest in mind. I trust You to lead me to ultimate mentors and to make me an ultimate mentor to someone else according to Your will. In the name of JESUS! AMEN!

Notes

Now the king was attracted to Esther more than to any of the other women, and she won his favor and approval more than any of the other virgins. So he set a royal crown on her head and made her queen instead of Vashti.

Esther 2:17

"Little did I realize, in the middle of the 1970s, that in less than a decade I would not only be back in Oklahoma working for my tribe, but I would be principal chief of the Cherokee Nation. I later learned that others did have that knowledge. Years before I was honored to become the first Cherokee woman chief, a Cherokee spiritual leader saw it all in visions as clear as spring water."

Wilma Mankiller

Principal Chief of the Cherokee Nation

(November 18, 1945 – April 6, 2010)

Chapter 4
Leaving the Harem

Consider a Greater Purpose
Vashti, Esther and the Courageous Women who Followed

One Night with the King

Just one night only! There would be no second chance. It is the moment we've all been waiting for! In the seventh year of the king's reign, Esther is summoned to have her one chance in the presence of King Xerxes. In the four years after Vashti's departure, he's seen a lot of young women. Esther won the favor of everyone who saw her. She walks with confidence as she is taken to the king's quarters with whatever items she decided to take from the harem. She had no other agenda than to please the king.

She holds Hegai's words close in her heart as she walks through the quiet, narrow and dim hallways. She exudes confidence, poise and beauty. Unknown to King Xerxes she also exudes the love of God. The sound of her footsteps gets softer and her pace slows down as she approaches the king's quarters. This is it! This is no fairy tale; Esther is in the presence of the king! This is her first encounter with the king. If only the walls could talk. Will the king call Esther's name or will she go back to the harem?

At first glance he knows she would be the next queen. He observes every inch of her body from head to toe. Esther was better than Vashti. His attraction for Esther is greater than any of the other young women. He is in awe of her beauty and how she carries herself. The beauty treatments prescribed for her paid off. It is an extraordinary moment.

Unlike today's paparazzi, news reports or social media of high profile breaking news, it is an intimate, private moment. It is hard to imagine that Esther met the king in privacy. King Xerxes was pleased with Esther and he wanted everybody else to know and celebrate with him. Word goes out to the 127 provinces, "The King Has a New Queen!"

Sometimes in life we only get one opportunity to do something—whether big or small—and our life is changed forever because of it. Sometimes these are planned situations and sometimes they are not. Both require leaving one set of circumstances to receive something else. It might even bring some discomfort, stress and hard work before receiving a desired outcome.

One of our most loved actresses in African-American film knows the pressure of only having one chance to prove yourself. Angela Bassett, who has played heroic roles of outstanding women such as Rosa Parks, Tina Turner and Betty Shabazz, told an audience at a 2013 *Women Empowerment* conference in Raleigh, North Carolina, about growing up in St. Petersburg, Florida. She shared how her own mother gave her two daughters opportunities to participate in school activities in preparation for their futures. Angela told how she was also encouraged by one of her teachers to attend Yale University, which her counselors had never encouraged her to consider. This teacher was only there for one year because he was called to active military duty, but he had planted a seed in her. She took his advice and later received a scholarship to attend the ivy-league university.

During the seven years at Yale Angela's greatest desire was to be in the drama club. The competition was fierce and she considered the hundreds of students who would apply. However, that didn't deter her. She would have only one chance to make an impression. Courage coupled with hard work included studying

Shakespeare and contemporary literature. It paid off! Her dream became a reality and opened doors for her to play a variety of roles not only at Yale, but on the big screen in Hollywood. That one chance made all the difference.

Chosen by the King

We are drawn into the room as the king slowly and carefully places the royal crown on Esther's head. She wears the crown, which was once worn by Vashti. Esther's life is about to change. It's the beginning of leaving the old and entering the new. When King Xerxes places the crown on Esther's head, he is saying she is the one! He affirms and validates her privately and publicly!

The importance of validation became personal to me when my leadership coach asked, "Were you validated when you first came to your church (as pastor)?" I thought about it. I knew the answer; however, I was caught off guard. No one had asked this question before. It was something I had not previously thought about, but I knew she was getting at something of importance.

I recall what I have since named, "The Meeting." It occurred in September 1999, just months after graduating from Columbia International University. I was hired as the co-pastor to serve along with the current pastor, who was also assuming the new title of co-pastor. Together, we served the only inner-city Christian Reformed church in Kalamazoo.

After a few weeks at my new church, I attended meetings with our pastors, elders and deacons in the region. The meeting began with an opening song. I was reminded that I was the only soprano and woman clergy among these tenor, bass and baritone voices. I was also the only dark-skinned person in the midst of this predominantly Dutch, male gathering.

I never questioned whether or not I belonged here. Before entering the sanctuary, I noticed several large portraits on the wall in the narthex. None of these serious faces looked like me. I wondered whether or not these men on the wall would be happy to see me in our denomination? Maybe some of them might.

Strange faces in the audience filled the room. At lunch I met a remarkable senior couple, who were advocates and champions for women in ministry. In the kitchen, I met women preparing to service tables. They greeted me with a smile, which put me at ease.

After lunch, the leaders gave an official introduction of me before I approached the platform. The platform was just a few steps from where I sat in the front row. However, mentally, the distance seemed like the length of a football field.

I confidently placed one foot in front of the other. My right foot touched the first of only two steps leading up to the platform. Before I spoke, I graciously took my position and paused. Standing at center stage, I looked over the audience as stillness and quietness filled the room. Their eyes were fixed on me with anticipation of what I would say. With confidence, poise and a smile, I said, "Praise the Lord! I am happy to accept the call as co-pastor of Immanuel Christian Reformed Church! I am glad to be here! I am a yielded vessel looking forward to serving God's people. I truly know that it was God who called me to the Christian Reformed Church and I am honored to be here."

Their hands came together clapping in concert. Many broke forth in a smile. I imagined a fellowship line for a friendly handshake or hug to take place. To me, this was my "Esther moment," the placing of a crown on my head. Although I was not crowned by an earthly king, our Heavenly King crowned me.

In several ways I was breaking ground in the Kalamazoo Christian Reformed churches and the denomination. I later learned about a division in our churches regarding women in the office of minister. That tension of division became an emotional strain for not only me, but for others. Needless to say, I continued to attend these quarterly meetings for about eight years. Later, I became more involved in our church's neighboring community. My professional relationship with these pastors remained in tack, in spite of theological differences.

When a person is accepted, affirmed and celebrated for their God-given gifts and calling, it makes all the difference. Acceptance is showing appreciation for a fellow servant in the Kingdom. It is not tolerance or a one-sided experience; it's a mutual appreciation. Affirmation releases us to fully participate and engage in ministry. It is acknowledging God for what He has done and being in agreement with His choice. Celebration is saying, "Yes, Lord," with an exclamation mark! Acceptance, affirmation and celebration are so crucial. The king's acceptance, affirmation and celebration were necessary for the new queen on a personal and communal level. King Xerxes felt good about his choice, and it was important for everybody to know this and embrace it.

Leaving the Harem

God was faithful in validating and giving me favor to serve as co-pastor for one year and sole pastor for twelve years. From the perspective of the neighboring and broader community, the installation service was quite affirming as people came together to witness God's work. I am truly blessed to have served thirteen years of uninterrupted, fruitful ministry with a great cloud of witnesses—above and below—cheering me on.

Acceptance, affirmation and celebration complement and speak loudly to what God is doing and saying within the body. All you have to do is pay attention to His work.

I asked a colleague to help me by suggesting the name of a Native American who has made a difference by courageously helping their people. With a strong sense of gratitude and pride he called out the name, Wilma Mankiller. I proceeded to research her to get a snapshot of her life. In her autobiography she said, "Especially in the context of a tribal people, no individual's life stands apart and alone from the rest. My own story has meaning only as long as it is a part of the overall story of my people." After reading these words, I felt a connection to Wilma.

Her story goes back to 1830, when the U.S. Congress passed the Indian Removal Act to relocate five Native American tribes from their land to form the Indian Territory west of the Mississippi River. Thousands of Native Americans were rushed off their ancestral native land so the government could claim ownership. The brutal takeover caused pain, suffering and death as they were literally marched away. Approximately 4,000 graves of loved ones and friends were scattered along what is called, "The Trail on Which We Cried" or "The Trail of Tears."

I held back my tears as I continued to read. The Native Americans not only were forced to leave their land, but as time went on they were forced to give up their native language and customs. This is a common practice when one group tries to dominate another less powerful (politically, emotionally or physically).

In 1945, the Mankillers gave birth to a baby girl named Wilma. When Wilma was a child, hard times led to the family's move from what is now Oklahoma to San Francisco. Wilma loved her people and creation. She realized the significance of her passion in the late 1960s when she participated in a demonstration at Alcatraz to bring awareness to the poor treatment of Native Americans. When her father died, his request was to be buried in the Mankiller Flats among his forefathers. It was during this time that Wilma's path in life became clearer as "she had felt the pull of the land." She had a burning desire to leave California and go back to her native land in Oklahoma to reclaim the land and help her people improve their quality of life. She left the commonplace to fulfill a specific purpose. Along the way she enrolled in the University of Arkansas where she earned a bachelor's degree in Social Science and a master's degree in Community Planning. These major accomplishments prepared Wilma to follow her path in grassroots work. Although she did not claim to be a Christian, her family regularly attended a Baptist church.

Her determination and preparedness opened doors. In 1983, at the age of 38, she was elected Deputy Chief of the Cherokee Nation; her running mate, Ross Swimmer, became Principal Chief. Although it was a difficult race, they won. Only two years later, Chief Swimmer took a national position, and Wilma accepted the great responsibility and honor of being the next chief. She was sworn in to complete two remaining years of the four-year term. Although there were some issues with her being a woman, she was respected and later elected to Chief of the Cherokee Nation after her interim position.

She was affirmed when she won that election. In turn she "revitalized" the nation. In numerous ways, she was recognized for her selfless contributions made to the Cherokee people and the entire world.

One of her greatest honors was when President Bill Clinton awarded Chief Mankiller with the Presidential Medal of Freedom in 1998—the highest award to a civilian by the United States government for their contributions in areas of national interests. Women who serve in male-dominated professions can certainly relate to one of Chief Mankiller's greatest honors. The seemingly small gesture of respect occurred at a memorial service being presided over by several male tribal elders.

The men invited her to sit with them in an area designated only for respected elders. This was the fullest extent of acceptance, affirmation and celebration that could be bestowed upon her. It is no surprise that one of Chief Mankiller's favorite songs was Aretha Franklin's "Respect." In April of 2010, the Chief died from pancreatic cancer.

Oftentimes, the right to sit with men in positions of authority is one that must be earned. By allowing a woman to sit in equal status says volumes for the contribution a woman makes to her society or career. While some great strides have been made in politics and business for women, the field of sports is another area growing to the acceptance of women and their contributions. The more than 80-year-old Augusta National Golf Club opened its once all-male membership to its first women members, Condoleezza Rice, former U.S. Secretary of State; and Darla Moore, a South Carolina philanthropist and entrepreneur.

Their acceptance of these women as members was validated shortly after they broke the decades-old barrier. At that year's annual pre-Masters opening (2012), chairman Billy Payne said of the historic memberships "This is a joyous occasion." He added, "This is a significant and positive time in our club's history and, on behalf of our membership, I wanted to take this opportunity to welcome them and all of our new members into the Augusta National family."

The Bible also shows us the significance of being affirmed and validated by the Body of Christ. It is an opportunity for the community to give its approval and blessings, whether in a physical or symbolic way. Moses validated Joshua, Barnabas validated Paul, and Paul validated Timothy. Mary McLeod Bethune validated Dorothy Height. Even in some Christian marriage ceremonies, the family, friends and community give their stamp of approval. Without it, we are left to fend for ourselves. The proof of acceptance is heard in our words and seen in our actions.

Even God validated His own Son after His baptism by John the Baptist. Can you imagine Heaven opening and the Spirit of God coming down like a dove on Jesus? God affirms by saying, "This is my Son, whom I love; with Him I am well pleased." It is made known to us that Jesus is God's Son, God loves Him, and He is well pleased with Him. God draws our attention to His work concerning His Son.

God favors His Son. Favor is like a stamp of approval. When you travel to another country the only way to enter is with a passport, an official stamp of approval. Once it is validated you are free to go on your way. When God gives favor it is a way of saying whose you are, who you are, and that He is pleased with you—His official stamp of approval. It's reason for giving thanks or to cry tears of joy.

Reflections

1. Can you think of a situation in which you only had one chance to make an impression? What went well? What did not?

2. How seriously do you take an opportunity as possibly being the only opportunity you might have to make a strong, positive impression in a situation? How might you prepare yourself in such a situation?

3. In what ways could you accept, affirm and celebrate others?

4. What thoughts come to mind when you think about God's favor shown in your life and your family?

5. As women of courage, what are some of the greatest barriers that hinder us from accepting God's favor in non-traditional roles and places?

Prayer
Heavenly Father, only You make it possible for us to be exalted to a new situation in life. We will take each opportunity seriously and look to You to help us along the way. Even when others reject us, we know wholeheartedly that we are accepted, affirmed and celebrated by You. You will always send others to help us wherever You have opened the door. What door You open, only You can close. What door You close, only You can open. We welcome new opportunities with Your blessings and leave unnecessary attitudes, traditions, lies, insecurities and inappropriate longings behind. Along the way, we will encourage and bless other women and girls who recognize Your hand at work in their lives to remain faithful to You and their calling. In the name of Jesus Christ.
AMEN

Notes

And the king gave a great banquet, Esther's banquet, for all his nobles and officials. He proclaimed a holiday throughout the provinces and distributed gifts with royal liberality.

Esther 2:18

"Whenever I met Mother, all self-consciousness left me. I felt right away at ease. She radiated peace and joy, even when she shared with me the darkness in her spiritual life. I was often amazed that someone who lived so much face to face with suffering people and went through a dark night herself, still could smile and make you feel happy....I believe that I can say that I felt in God's presence, in the presence of truth and love…"

**Words of Father Michael van der Peet
Congregation of the Priests of the Sacred Heart about
Mother Teresa of Calcutta**

(August 26, 1910 – February 5, 1997)

Chapter 5
In the Presence of Royalty

Truly Royalty

King Xerxes has an abundance of everything! He reigns from his royal throne. The royal wine is abundant and served in individually unique goblets of gold. His giving is in royal liberality. Royal officials guard the gates and royal secretaries scribe fluently in other languages to the people in royal provinces. Monies are given to his royal treasury. The royal couple wears royal crowns and garments. His couriers ride royal horses. The king's possessions make a powerful statement about him--he's got status, power and sovereignty. He invites the Who's Who of all 127 provinces to celebrate his new queen.

Esther has a new beginning, a new life unlike anything she has ever experienced. Out of all the young women up for the position he chose her to be the queen. Whatever the queen needs, she can expect to get it. She has several royal robes to choose from and a staff to attend to her every request and privilege. She soon will learn even more about the perks of being royalty.

We are truly royalty because we belong to God. It is in Jesus Christ that we become new; our character is transformed to be like Him.

This is what Father van der Peet saw in Mother Teresa every time they met, the Christ in her. From what I've seen of her on television or read about in magazines and books, Mother Teresa is one of the most humble people I have ever heard of. The work she began in one of the poorest parts of the world, Calcutta, India, brought light to those who had no hope. She never took credit for this work. In fact, she considered herself as nothing.

In the Presence of Royalty

She simply had a big heart for Jesus and honored his teachings and suffering for our sin, in her ministry to serve the suffering.

Although she may not have understood why God called her to a life of poverty and to serve the poorest of the poor, she took joy in serving the King. In regard to the work, she said, "We shall bring them to Christ and Christ to them." Being in the presence of royalty is more than an emotional expression. When we are in His presence what we give to others reflects who He is.

Patty Reed told of an experience while in the Ukraine on a mission trip. She and her team visited a home for single mothers. She and her team were invited to pray and fellowship in the rooms of the mothers. However, Patty and two friends remained in the hallway to pray for the place, for those being prayed for in each room and all Ukrainian women. A Ukrainian woman approached them and asked them to go with her to two rooms to pray for the women and their children. While praying in the second room the Lord impressed in Patty's spirit that she "was standing in the presence of princesses." Isaiah 62:3 came to her: *You will be a crown of splendor in the Lord's hand, a royal diadem in the hand of your God.*

She was overwhelmed by this truth and honored to pray for them. She "was praying over princesses, beautiful daughters of the King that He adores." She felt "compelled to be sure they knew that they were truly royalty." These young ladies had very little possessions, but they were truly royalty. They belonged to the King. We can imagine how these young ladies must have felt after being told this. They had been given a new beginning when they became daughters of the King.

The same applies for each one of us. No matter what circumstances we come from, He adores us.

Those who are predestined to be the King's treasured possession acquire royalty. What others see in us ought to leave a positive impression of who God is. He is the King of the ages, the Eternal King, the Great King, and the King of Glory. He reigns over everything. He is establishing His Kingdom on earth as it is in Heaven.

While we were given a new beginning in a physical life of royalty, we are given a new beginning (spiritual life) in the presence of royalty when we become born again. We are royalty! *You will be called a new name that the mouth of the Lord will bestow,"* (Isaiah 62:2b). A new beginning starts with an encounter with the King of Kings and Lord of Lords.

My new beginning in the presence of royalty came in 1988, when I was personally summoned by the King of Kings and Lord of Lords. He called me out of darkness into His marvelous presence to live forever. He gave me a new name–Christian, the family of God and it is an experience I hope to never forget.

As a child and young adult I was quite aware of God, but I didn't *know* Him. When I was 29 years old I felt like something was missing in my life. I wasn't married (which was alright); I had male friends (which also was alright). I describe this time of my life as being empty and unfulfilled.

Several years later God became real to me. Without any plans for what happened next, I came home from work, set down my briefcase, fell on my knees and asked Jesus to come into my heart. He did.

Ironically, weeks before, a close friend had talked to me about having an intimate personal relationship with Jesus Christ. I thought he was crazy at the time. He asked me to read one of the gospels and a book called *The God You Can Know,* by Dan DeHaan. My life was never the same after reading DeHaan's book. That evening when I became born again, I was filled with joy as tears ran down my face. All my sins were forgiven in that moment and I knew it! There is no greater joy than to belong to Jesus Christ and to know His love. There is no king like our King!

King Xerxes rules 127 provinces; the entire kingdom belongs to God.

King Xerxes sits on a man-made throne; God sits on a heavenly throne robed in majesty.

King Xerxes gives liberally; "For God so loved the world that he gave His one and only Son, that whoever believes in Him shall not perish but have eternal life." (John 3:16)

King Xerxes is indecisive; he needed counsel from his law experts. God needs no counsel. There is no one who enlightens or understands Him.

Consider a Greater Purpose
Vashti, Esther and the Courageous Women who Followed

I had grown up in the church and was baptized when I was 8 years old. But at that moment, in the privacy of my own home, I was brought into an intimate, personal relationship with Him. He walks with me. He talks with me. I know that I belong to Him. I know that I am a part of His body. I know He loves me no matter what. I know He has a plan for my life and that plan is good. I hope my response is always, "Yes, Lord."

After asking Jesus to come into my life I chose not to get rebaptized, but I made a public recommitment to the Lord that I will live for Him all the days of my life. It was a wonderful celebration of His grace and mercy for a sinner like me. I could relate to a line in the song, "Amazing Grace" by John Newton, which says, "How precious did that Grace appeared, the hour I first believed."

> *King Xerxes has a royal treasure; we are God's royal priesthood and treasured possessions. Psalm 65:4 says, "Blessed are those You choose and bring near to live in Your courts! We are filled with the good things of Your house, of Your holy temple."*
>
> *King Xerxes could rewrite his decrees; God's royal decrees cannot be changed.*
>
> *King Xerxes is finite; God is the King eternal, immortal, invisible, and the only God.*
>
> *The King of Kings and Lord of Lords is far greater than any earthly king. Esther was in the presence of a great man, whom she would grow to love and respect, but she did not worship him.*

In the Presence of Royalty

Years later, when I was attending seminary, a chapel speaker mentioned that his friend Dan DeHaan, a church youth minister, had once attended our school. On February 19, 1982, Dan was killed when a plane he was flying crashed. He was just 39 years old. Although Dan is with the Lord now, others are still being brought into the Kingdom through his witness. I never met Dan, but he is an example of how we personally may never know how many people we bring to the Kingdom through our witness. Dan's book was instrumental in my walk, which led to me later enrolling in seminary. Praise the Lord!

King Xerxes invited everyone to celebrate his new queen. We are invited to the King's table to sup (have fellowship) with Him and be His witnesses in Jerusalem, Judea, Samaria and the uttermost parts of the world! We are people of His eternal Kingdom!

A Heart for Worship

The words royalty and majesty are similar. Both are associated with worship in the scriptures—in particular the Psalms. Despite her new status and position, Esther, like Mordecai, may have never stopped worshiping God. We, too, were created to worship our King. When we have a true perspective of what it means to be His daughters, we worship Him liberally.

The act of worship is "to pay homage or, literally, to ascribe worth to some person or thing." Psalm 95 says, *Come, let us worship and bow down. Let us kneel before the LORD our maker.* The attitude of our heart and obedience are important to God. Psalm 51:16-17 reads, *You do not delight in sacrifice, or I would bring it; you do not take pleasure in burnt offerings. The sacrifices of God*

Consider a Greater Purpose
Vashti, Esther and the Courageous Women who Followed

are a broken spirit; a broken and contrite heart, O God, you will not despise. Psalm 34:18 reads, *The Lord is close to the brokenhearted and saves those who are crushed in spirit.* We are privileged to worship our great God 24/7 no matter where we are.

A beautiful story about a woman who presses her way through to worship Jesus is noteworthy. Some scholars believe it was Mary Magdalene. She didn't hesitate to go to a Pharisee's house where Jesus was having dinner, just to be in His presence. Mary did what most women of her day would never have done, but Jesus loved to be with repentant sinners, even women. It made no difference to Him that she was known as a sinful woman.

She stood behind Jesus with feelings of unworthiness as she entered with an alabaster jar of perfume into the company of men. Tears fell from her eyes onto His feet and she began to wipe them with her hair as she poured perfume on them. Mary was in the presence of royalty. Jesus points out that what she did was a demonstration of the greatness of her love for the Savior. She had a big heart for Jesus! When we have a big heart for Jesus, our worship is true and we are not in bondage to what other people think about us.

Mary knew she wasn't the same woman she used to be. I felt the same way when I was saved! As Mary shows us, it can be an emotional experience, but it is more than an emotional or physical encounter. Mary knew she had a transforming encounter with Jesus. He affirmed her in the midst of a group of religious people. No one ever knew that this same woman who loved Jesus so much would be the first one to see the Risen Savior in the garden, where He called her by name!

In the Presence of Royalty

Vocalist Cece Winans captures the sentiment of Mary's gratitude:

Mary's Alabaster Box
And I've come to pour My praise on Him
Like oil from Mary's Alabaster box.
Don't be angry if I wash His feet with my tears
and I dry them with my hair.
You weren't there the night He found me.
You did not feel what I felt
when He wrapped His love all around me.
And you don't know the cost of the oil
In my Alabaster box.

> *In what ways do you have to press your way through to worship Him? What are you willing to risk?*
>
> *What is the cost of the oil in your Alabaster box?*

Worship is personal or corporate, and a vertical and horizontal encounter. God reveals Himself to us. There is a giving and receiving component in worship, but it is primarily about giving God honor and glory. In the book of Isaiah 66:1-2 it says: *This is what the Lord says: 'Heaven is My throne, and the earth is My footstool. Where is the house you will build for Me? Where will My resting place be? Has not My hand made all these things, and so they came into being? declares the Lord. This is the one I esteem: he who is humble and contrite in spirit, and trembles at My word.'*

We see God sitting on His throne high above the universe with His feet relaxing on the earth, which is His ottoman. He and the angelic hosts are looking down at the earth. God tells them, "I made all of this—everything for My glory!" He says, "Look over there," as He points to a woman who is reading her Bible with an open heart and a conviction to obey his word. She's in His presence. She becomes aware of something in her life that does not align with His will as she reads His word.

God says to the angels, "She's got my attention; I'll help her." While she's praying, she senses an agreement in her spirit and has peace within her trouble. She then bows on her knees and praises His name. She's in His presence. In John 4:24, He looks for those who worship Him in spirit and in truth. We don't have to worry or be frustrated about our shortcomings; the Holy Spirit will help us. He is our Helper. God delights in His children giving Him all the glory.

One of the most famous African-American women in the 19th century was Sojourner Truth. She advocated and preached for human rights. She, too, had an encounter with the King. She is recorded saying that God revealed Himself to her, with all the suddenness of a flash of lightning. She said it was like He was showing her, in the twinkling of an eye, that He was all over—that He pervaded the universe —and that there was no place He was not.

I understand her statement completely. One day I was driving when the song, "When I Think About the Lord" by Hillsong United came on my radio. I had to pull off the road to take in the awesome praise through the words:

> *"...how He saved me,*
> *how He raised me,*
> *how He filled me with the Holy Ghost,*
> *how He healed me to the uttermost."*

I couldn't hold back the tears as I cried out to our awesome, Holy God! There's nothing wrong with an emotional experience as an expression of gratitude, but it must lead to obedience! After Sojourner's encounter with God she lived fearlessly in her fight against slavery and for women's rights. Thinking about what's in your Alabaster box, what you sacrifice for Him, can have a moving effect on you.

Remember, we live in the presence of royalty when we daily live in His presence. As the psalmist says in Psalm 84:10, *Better is one day in Your courts than a thousand elsewhere; I rather be a doorkeeper in the house of my God than dwell in the tents of the wicked.*

The psalmist is saying that he would rather be on the inside of the temple versus being on the outside in the tents of the wicked; a representation of ungodliness. On the inside of the temple is where the presence of God dwells. For us, being in His presence is not connected to a physical place but an internal dwelling. God's Spirit dwells within you.

Consider a Greater Purpose
Vashti, Esther and the Courageous Women who Followed

Without Him, you would not be able to experience the joy of His presence. In His presence, there is fullness of joy. In His presence, He fills our cup with everything we need --love, joy, peace, patience, kindness, goodness, faithfulness, gentleness and self-control. He is satisfying. Through the Holy Spirit, God makes it possible for us to always be in His presence. Is there anywhere else you would rather be than every moment in His courts? As I wrote on my Facebook page one morning, "Simply enjoying His presence." Everything wasn't going smoothly, but it didn't make a difference. I was in His presence where there is joy and peace.

One morning I tuned in to the Christian radio program on Kalamazoo's 1560 The Touch. While it was on I was trying to do some light housework. I tuned in to the words of the gospel song, "I Need Your Glory." I listened closely to the next few words from the song by Ernest Pugh:

> *I need your Glory, I want your Glory,*
> *Less of me and more of you is what I need,*
> *Show me your Glory,*
> *And show me your power,*
> *Less of me and more of you is what I need.*

I believe the songwriter is saying, "I want to align with God's will in obedience." I've learned that when I'm in His glory, it changes me. I am more like Christ and willing to follow Him wherever He leads.

Ernest Pugh's got it right. We need His glory so that there is less of us, and more of Him. This is not a light request! I believe during Esther's preparation, she became less of self and more of God because His fingerprints were on this situation.

In the Presence of Royalty

One of the greatest gifts we can give to our children is to make sure they know what it means to be in the presence of the Lord. It's more than attending a worship service, lifting Holy hands and saying, "Hallelujah!" It is also about what happens after you leave the church.

When someone is in your presence, don't you acknowledge them? When someone is in your presence, don't you listen to what they have to say and respond? I'm talking about being captivated by the Almighty God. He gets your attention. Through this encounter, we believe and value what pleases Him. It doesn't mean you are perfect. Psalm 37:23-24 (NLT) says, *The steps of the godly are directed by the Lord. He delights in every detail of their lives. Though they stumble, they will not fall, for the Lord holds them by the hand.* To be in His presence means He is directing your life.

You sense His leading because He communicates His will in a way that you understand, or until you understand. You may make some mistakes in the journey of life, but He keeps you from falling down by holding your hand. Recovering from a stumble might take time, but it is better than going completely down.

Reflections

1. Describe what being in the presence of the "King" means to you. What difference does it make in your life? How does it affect those people around you?

2. Give a specific example of when His presence is (was) real to you.

3. How can you help others experience the reality of living in royalty?

4. What is the Holy Spirit asking of you personally about living in royalty?

5. When you encounter other "royal princesses and queens," how open are you to encouraging and blessing them as a reminder of whose they are?

Prayer
Father, You are greater than all other kings. There is none like You. Your kingdom endures forever. Without Your presence we are lifeless, powerless and empty. Without Your presence we walk in darkness. In Your presence we receive true light and abundant life. We are witnesses of Your faithful love and blessed hope. We are able to stand against the evil forces of this world and to be strong witnesses for Jesus Christ because You are here with us. We want to be mindful of Your presence at all times. It's in the name of JESUS CHRIST we pray. AMEN

Notes

During the time Mordecai was sitting at the king's gate, Bigthana and Teresh, two of the king's officers who guarded the doorway, became angry and conspired to assassinate King Xerxes. But Mordecai found out about the plot and told Queen Esther, who in turn reported it to the king, giving credit to Mordecai.

Esther 2:21-22

"In the concentration camp where I was imprisoned many years ago, sometimes bitterness and hatred tried to enter my heart when people were so cruel to my sister and me. Then I learned this prayer (based on) Romans 5:5.

Thank You, Lord Jesus, that You have brought into my heart the love of God through the Holy Spirit, who is given to me. Thank You, Father, that Your love in me is victorious over the bitterness in me and cruelty around me.

After I prayed it, I experienced the miracle that there was no room for bitterness in my heart any more. Will you learn to pray that prayer too? If you are a child of God, you have a great task in your prison. You are a representative of the Lord Jesus, the King of kings."

Corrie ten Boom – Preacher and Writer

Nazi Concentration Camp Survivor

(April 15, 1892 – April 15, 1983)

Chapter 6
The Presence of Evil in the Palace

Consider a Greater Purpose
Vashti, Esther and the Courageous Women who Followed

Allegiance with the King

Esther's life has become much like a fairy tale little girls dream of. She is a beautiful young woman who has been taken from her modest home to the king's palace where he falls in love with her at first sight and makes her his queen. And, everything is happy thereafter...well, not quite. Esther has not yet revealed her Jewish heritage.

In the meantime, Mordecai continues to make his daily visits to the king's gate. One day, his routine pays off. It is at the gate that he overhears a conspiracy to kill the king. Bigthana and Teresh, who were the king's officers guarding the doorway, plot to do away with him to deal with their anger. Mordecai gets the word to the queen (probably by one of the young women in the harem) and Queen Esther tells the king.

After the plot was confirmed, King Xerxes had Bigthana and Teresh hanged on the gallows. The king ensured these events were recorded in the annals while he was present.

> ***The Esther reading group response:***
>
> ***Mordecai is fearless, passionate, wise and loyal to his principles. He wouldn't bow down to Haman.***

The Presence of Evil in the Palace

Prior to this, Mordecai's name meant nothing to the king. Mordecai's allegiance went beyond Xerxes. It is part of Persian history. He was also loyal to his God.

Mordecai and Queen Esther desire to do what is right in the eyes of God and to circumvent the devil's work. Their allegiance to the king is proven to be real. Also this is the kind of loyalty we should desire for one another. We should long for it. For some allegiance is conditional, based on selfish outcomes that oftentimes are short-lived and unfruitful.

The loyalty given to the king resembles our loyalty to God. One of my favorite encouragers, Cornelia "Corrie" ten Boom, demonstrated a deep sense of loyalty to God, even when she was informed that all her family members were killed. Corrie was a prisoner in Ravensbruck concentration camp during World War II because she and her family helped rescue and hide Jews from the Nazis. Places like Ravensbruck seemed to harbor evil. All ten of her family members died in various Nazi concentration camps—except her. Corrie was released due to a clerical error.

I learned about how courageous a woman Corrie was a couple years after coming to know Jesus Christ as Lord and Savior. I was attending a meeting with leaders in the Fellowship of Christian Athletics (FCA) in Lansing, Michigan, where a friend and I met with three other couples. After our initial introduction, the men went in one room and the women in another.

It was then that a conversation began about this Dutch woman by the name of Corrie ten Boom. They recommended one of her books that told about her experience being arrested by

German officials. Through her extraordinary bravery while being in prison, I learned the beauty of staying true to God in all situations. Corrie was truly loyal to her Lord.

Corrie says, "Never be afraid to trust an unknown future to a known God." She admits that at times she was afraid, but she remembered her God and never turned her back on Him. By God's grace, Corrie survived the concentration camps. She called herself "a tramp for the Lord," meaning that she tramped the world carrying the good news. She served years as His servant, until her health required confinement to the bed.

Loyalty is being faithful regardless of any "temptation to renounce, desert, or betray." True disciples of Jesus Christ will try with the help of the Holy Spirit not to give into the temptation to turn our back on God and the things of God. If only for a moment, we will come back. Those who are loyal to God will always turn back to Him even in messy, sinful situations. What's beautiful about turning back to God is that you can be honest with Him—no manipulation, just pure honesty and the naked truth.

Loyalty to one's family unfolds beautifully in the book of Ruth between a mother-in-law, Naomi, and a daughter-in-law, Ruth. The story takes place during the time of the judges. Naomi, her husband and two sons move to Moab because there was a famine in Judah. The sons, Mahlon and Kilion, married women from their new homeland named Orpah and Ruth. Naomi's husband died and ten years later so did her sons. All three women were widowed and uncertain about their futures.

The Presence of Evil in the Palace

When Naomi heard that the famine had ended in Judah she headed back, taking her daughter-in-laws with her. However, Naomi begs the women to return to their homeland, not knowing what the future held for the women in a foreign land. With tears in her eyes, Orpah kissed her goodbye. Ruth, however, remains, vowing to take care of her mother-in-law saying, *Don't urge me to leave you or to turn back from you. Where you go I will go, and where you stay I will stay. Your people will be my people and your God my God. Where you die I will die, and there I will be buried. May the Lord deal with me, be it ever so severely, if even death separates you and me* (Ruth 1:16-17).

Fast forward back in Judah…Ruth meets Boaz while gleaning in the fields. He gives Ruth favor by allowing her to glean in his fields during harvest time, taking enough to provide for Naomi. Through God's providence in their lives, Boaz marries Ruth and they have a son, Obed, who is the father of Jesse, the father of David. Ruth's loyalty to Naomi became the catalyst used by God to bless them beyond measure.

A New Man on the Scene

Who is this guy? He comes out of nowhere. He was probably one of the king's officials, but he is elevated to a higher office than any of the other nobles. His name is Haman, son of Hammedatha, the Agagite. He must be someone pretty important as he feels everyone should bow down to him. Mordecai does not stoop so low. He is bold, fearless and a Jew. He knows there could be a price to pay for disobeying the king's orders to bow to Haman, but he isn't overly concerned.

Consider a Greater Purpose
Vashti, Esther and the Courageous Women who Followed

Haman refuses to be "dissed" (slang for disrespected) by this Jew. If others find out about this lack of respect they may mock him and chose not to bow either. Haman has two options: to tolerate Mordecai or to show his authority. He chooses the latter and plans to kill Mordecai and all the Jewish people in all 127 provinces. How drastic!

Mordecai posed a threat to Haman's power each time he refused to bow to him. Just picture Mordecai turning his head away from Haman. The longer Haman stared at Mordecai the deeper his resentment and anger became. Those evil thoughts lingered in Haman's heart that would lead to no good.

> ***Who does Haman represent in this role?***

Sometimes people can make it difficult for us if we are not in agreement with them, their methods, ideologies, etc. They fear losing something important to them like power, control or resources. The reality is that there are some Haman-types in our families, workplaces, communities, schools, political arenas and even churches. They try everything possible whether consciously or subconsciously to get rid of you or to hinder you from flowing in your calling, giftedness and assignment. Driven by personal beliefs and values contrary to your own, they may make it miserable for you and others. They will hold back information or always be in disagreement with you. None of us are exempt from these kinds of people.

> *The Esther reading group response:*
>
> *Haman is hungry for power, evil and self-centered. Other distinguishing characteristics of evil, as we look at Haman, are detestable, vindictive, cunning, bad influence, intolerant and unworthy of honor. He is bad news for the Jews.*

Not so long ago, Rhonda A. Lee, a young meteorologist who is African American, lost her job. The firing was the result of her responding to an offensive remark put on the KTBS 3 News' Facebook page (an affiliate of ABC in Shreveport, Louisiana).

The man who made the comment said, "The black lady that does the news is a very nice lady. The one thing is she needs to wear is a wig or grow some more hair. I'm not sure if she is a cancer patient."

The station did not respond. After several days, Lee responded, "I'm very proud of who I am and the standard of beauty I display. Women come in all shapes, sizes, nationalities and levels of beauty…"

Consider a Greater Purpose
Vashti, Esther and the Courageous Women who Followed

The KTBS 3 News' policy states that its "employees must not respond to social media comments." Lee claims this policy was previously never conveyed to her. She got a "pink slip" instead. Lee had no regrets. The following year, she accepted a meteorology position with Weather National in Denver.

No matter what happens to us, we know God is still in control. We also know who is really behind an unjust act: Satan. He gets upset when you do God's will. When your enemies try to harm you, they are really fighting God. *Put on the full armor of God, so that you can take your stand against the devil's schemes. For our struggle is not against flesh and blood, but against the rulers, against the authorities, against the powers of this dark world and against the spiritual forces of evil in the heavenly realms* (Ephesians 6:11-12). Don't get mad at the vessel used for evil deeds. Pray for them.

In the fifth year of Queen Esther's crowning and the twelfth year and the first month of King Xerxes' reign, Haman tells the king about this "certain people" that should be killed. He never mentions that his enemy is the Jews and he trusts and respects Haman's opinion, not realizing the origin of this vendetta. Haman claimed that the Jews would threaten the kingdom by having an influence on Persians. The threat to the kingdom is similar to their concern for the officials' wives being influenced by Queen Vashti's disobedience —totally unfounded.

A lot is cast to determine when the mass murder would occur. The good news is that it would not happen immediately but in the twelfth month. God and time are on the Jews' side. In the meantime, the king seals the edict with his signet ring and tops it off with a celebration drinking with Haman.

The Presence of Evil in the Palace

> *The Esther reading group response:*
>
> *We questioned the king's decision to go along with a mass murder. He did not question Haman.*

At this point, Mordecai is unaware of Haman's scheme to get rid of his people. More than being "the enemy of the Jews," Haman is the enemy of God. However, the news soon spreads. If the Jews are a problem, why don't the people know it? The Persians are "bewildered" and soon Mordecai hears of the edict. The bad news brings on a cataclysmic response filled with loud wailing and sorrow.

Mordecai tears his clothing, covering himself with sackcloth and ashes. He is more concerned about others than himself and recognizes his role in this death sentence for the Jews. The pain is so deep it was unbearable. Mordecai wonders what he has done. He thinks about those he put in harm's way. If only he could turn back the hands of time.

Word gets to Esther about the mental state of her cousin. She responds in great distress not knowing the cause of his sorrow. Out of love and concern she sends clothes for Mordecai, but he refuses them and continues to grieve. He moves from standing on the outside of the king's gate, to the open square of the city in front of the king's gate. Still, Queen Esther persists. This time she sends one of her eunuchs, Hathach, to find out what's going on. Queen Esther knew nothing about the rift between Mordecai and Haman. Mordecai tells Hathach everything. He is proactive and takes responsibility for his actions.

After some deep thought he feels helpless, but not hopeless. He is a capable, smart man, but his hands are tied. He never badmouthed his enemy, Haman. He had a plan, but Esther had to carry it through. He wants Hathach to explain the copy of the edict to her and urge her to go to the king and plead for the lives of her people.

Dr. Bechtel in her commentary on Esther makes an important point that Queen Esther's response was that Mordecai was in the open square. It makes you wonder what she was thinking at the time. Was she concerned about keeping her identity unknown or about Mordecai's safety?

Mordecai became a person of interest to Esther's maids and eunuchs because they knew about their secret. This tells us that they have a trusting relationship with the queen.

Dr. Bechtel says concerning the queen's isolation that the edict originated from inside of the palace, but the queen had no knowledge of it. If she had known about it, she would have been looking for Mordecai from the beginning. It's frightening to think about how easy it is to live in our own palaces oblivious to the problems on the outside of our gated communities. Physical boundaries can sometimes keep us from getting to know and understand the problems of the people on the outside. It's too easy to ignore the challenges in other communities if we

The Presence of Evil in the Palace

live in isolation. You have to be interested in what's going on outside of the palace to know what's going on in the streets of Susa.

What does this mean for Queen Esther?

Reflections

1. On a scale of one to five (one being the lowest) how loyal are you? To whom are you loyal?

2. How do you impose your need to be honored by others? What should you do instead?

3. How aware are you of spiritual warfare? How do you respond to it?

4. In what ways do you make an effort in knowing what is happening in your own community? What about the global community?

5. How might God use you in reaching out to those outside of a gated community? What's on your heart?

Prayer

Father, help me to be loyal to the people You have placed in my life. May I not engage in conversations or schemes with the intent of discrediting someone else's name. Give me wisdom and discernment to know when someone is pulling me in a direction that does not show my allegiance to the people placed in my life to build me up. Help me to show my loyalty by standing up when someone or something is trying to pull them down. Give me the courage and words to speak up against those things that bring harm to innocent people. Above all things help me to be obedient to Your Spirit. In the powerful name of Jesus, AMEN.

Notes

Then Esther sent this reply to Mordecai: 'Go, gather together all the Jews who are in Susa, and fast for me. Do not eat or drink for three days, night or day. I and my maids will fast as you do. When this is done, I will go to the king, even though it is against the law. And if I perish, I perish.' So Mordecai went away and carried out all of Esther's instructions.

Esther 4:15-17

"A few days after my decision to become a Jesus-follower, God performed a miracle that reinforced my commitment. Jing Zhang's organization, Women's Rights in China, which Bob and I support, had reunited a young woman with her family 25 years after she was kidnapped at age seven. When the news came, the entire village, which had witnessed the parents' years of tears and heartbreak, rushed to the train station to greet the lost daughter."

Chai Ling

**Founder of All Girls Allowed
("In Jesus Name, Simply Love Her")**

Author of *A Heart for Freedom*

Chapter 7
The Beauty and Strength of Community

Consider a Greater Purpose
Vashti, Esther and the Courageous Women who Followed

The Request to Save God's People

Saving his people becomes Mordecai's greatest concern as he stands at the king's gate—the barrier between him and Queen Esther. He could not go any further than the gate because he was dressed in sackcloth. Great mourning among the Jews went beyond the gate to the 127 provinces as they submitted themselves to weeping and wailing to their God. They pray that He hears the cries of His people and responds, quickly.

Hathach goes back to Queen Esther with Mordecai's plan to save the Jews. She quickly realizes that approaching the king without being summoned is a risk. On a more personal note, she reveals that the king has not called her to come before him in the last thirty days.

> **We don't really know what's going on with the king and Queen Esther, but the romance has simmered down. Too many writers have given a negative opinion concerning Esther's response. The queen is perceived as being self-centered and insensitive to the issue at hand.**

This is where I would like to rewrite the script. Queen Esther could have used some encouragement and support. Did Mordecai think Esther forgot where she came from? Did he forget how much love she has for her own people? Esther merely states the facts; she doesn't say she is not willing to take the risk. Once again, the Jews have God and time on their side. Like the young folks say, "It is what it is." Imagine being in Esther's shoes. This is not a little thing she is being asked to do. She's a realist. Maybe she needs more time to think it through. Esther's mind is taken back to an old question when she was first brought to the king's harem. "Why am I here?"

> **Esther reading group response:**
>
> **Esther probably thought about the risk taken by Vashti when she refused the king. Now, Esther is about to break the law by going to the king.**

God made it possible for Mordecai to learn about Haman's plot to kill him and the entire Jewish people. Although Mordecai did not have access to Queen Esther, who is the only one positioned to save them, her maids and eunuchs came with the message about Mordecai and other Jews laying in sackcloth and ashes.

Queen Esther became very concerned when Mordecai refused to take off the sackcloth and put on clean clothes and sends Hathach, one of the king's eunuchs, to act as the liaison.

Chai Ling, author of *A Heart for Freedom,* tells of her passion early in life to help free the Chinese people when she lived there. Chai was chosen as the commander-in-chief of a nonviolent student movement called the Defend Tiananmen Square Headquarters, which was "rooted in a simple demand that all people be treated with justice and dignity."

Consider a Greater Purpose
Vashti, Esther and the Courageous Women who Followed

Without warning, on June 4, 1989, these protesters were overpowered by the Beijing military and thousands of students were killed. It became known as the Tiananmen Massacre. The students were not armed. The officials went looking for Chai. She wondered, "Why am I still alive?" She lived in exile in Beijing until she escaped to Hong Kong by hiding in a cargo boxcar for 105 hours. She was one of the top Most Wanted students in Beijing. A passion for the people she left behind never changed.

Within a short period of time she made connections through the University of Hong Kong to become a refugee in the United States or France. She later came to the United States.

Although Chai was broken when she arrived in New York City, she was quickly connected with government officials who knew about her past. Doors were opened as she became part of a caring community, but still struggled with what happened in Tiananmen Square, the separation from her family and difficulties in making the adjustments of being in another country. Through the China Initiative, she received a scholarship to study at Princeton University and eventually earned a decent salary and felt accepted by the broader community.

Chai's story tells of God's grace through a series of events. A three-hour prayer meeting was held to pray for the students who died in Tiananmen and for peace in China. During that service, her new friends were praying for Jesus to come into her heart. Although Chai was firm in her Buddhist faith, she was impressed by the service. She was moved by a sermon about God's purpose in your life and leaving a legacy. The message

The Beauty and Strength of Community

shared how temporal things do not satisfy the void in our hearts that can only be filled by God's love.

A woman named Reggie Littlejohn, president of Women's Rights Without Frontiers, had a profound impression on Chai. She was impressed by her "humility and confident assurance." Littlejohn, a Christian, had a passion for eliminating "forced abortions under the one-child policy." Everything about Reggie's life was about Jesus. God even planted some seeds through a book read by Chai about a young Christian man whose legs were broken to keep him from escaping prison after being arrested because of his faith.

Chai had lots of questions and wonderings about God. As she contemplated this new belief and spoke more with Reggie, God gave Chai a vision to "bring God's love to China." Right in Chai's office on the 35th floor of the Prudential Building, she accepted Jesus into her life after bowing on her knees in humble submission to His purpose for her life. She gave up the reigns.

The Women's Rights in China, with God's help, successfully brought a "lost daughter" back to her family after twenty-five years of being in a kidnap situation. Chai's purpose was reaffirmed.

Chai Ling is an incredible woman of God. She is courageous and committed to bring God's love to China by restoring the lives of young girls and women who are imprisoned by social injustices. God is using a community to set free the captives.

Consider a Greater Purpose
Vashti, Esther and the Courageous Women who Followed

The Need for Fasting and Prayer

Queen Esther helps us to see the beauty and strength of community. After she understands the seriousness of this situation, she doesn't say, "I've got this!" No, she tells Hathach to inform Mordecai to, "Go, gather together all the Jews who are in Susa, and fast for me." This request also demonstrates Esther's strength. She values fasting and prayer. She doesn't act like the Lone Ranger or a Superwoman, feeling she can handle it herself. The beauty and strength of community come across loud and clear as Esther initiates the call for everyone to be in one accord.

Sometimes we become so action oriented that we fail to consider God, and the importance of gathering a community in prayer. We forget to seek God's help or neglect to allow others to join in intercession. It takes a submissive spirit to acknowledge how much we need Him, and it is powerful when it happens in community.

Esther's initiative shows a dependency on God and His people by calling for a fast, which is usually accompanied with prayer. I admire this about Esther. She is saying, we are in this together and need each other. It also sends a message to God of how much Esther needs His help, strength, courage and wisdom.

God just loves it when we need Him. He waits for us to say, "Lord, we need You." We can tell Him what we need and believe He will answer us. The fact that He already knows what we need should not keep us from going to Him. The discipline of fasting and prayer is something we should practice often. God can take

The Beauty and Strength of Community

care of all our doubts and fears. Those prayers will help sustain us and give us a sense of peace.

In addition, the beauty and strength of community in times of crisis is powerful. When our needs cause us to look beyond barriers that tend to separate us under normal situations like faith, tradition, race and socioeconomics, we rise to the occasion. Esther's request crossed a barrier; it brought the Gentiles and Jews together for a good cause.

I was so blessed to serve as pastor to one of the most caring churches I have ever known. They taught me the beauty and strength of community. This became even more evident years later. Immanuel Church in Kalamazoo is not a church building or congregation; it is a family. It is a body of believers who are bound by the love of Jesus Christ with a deep level of vulnerability and trust in God. This is a powerful testimony of what God was doing in a culturally and racially diverse community.

In another light, we know of mothers who took the lead and initiative to organize themselves around a pressing concern in their community. They put a plea out and other women responded. Prayer took place on a street corner or in a church because their children, sons and/or daughters, became victims of violence in the streets. They united with those who had experienced a similar tragedy in their own family. They needed each other for support, prayer and strength. They wanted to make a difference and a bold, unified statement.

They had the courage to stand up to say, "No more!" The depth of their pain and grief of losing a child sent them together to God in a plea, "Lord have mercy; save our children." What beauty and strength when a community comes together to plea to God on behalf of others.

> **Comments from the Esther reading group:**
>
> **Esther was the conduit to save her people. This was a real situation. She was a Jew and had to be saved too.**

The news from Hathach came to the queen on an ordinary day, which was interrupted with devastating news about her people's fate. Her first recorded words come as a cautious, deliberate voice. She's not a pushover. She is definitely misunderstood by Mordecai. He thinks being in the palace has made her insensitive to her own people. Maybe he thinks she's trying to save herself when he says, "Do not think that because you are in the king's house you alone of all the Jews will escape."

God is sustaining her and she knows it. However, Mordecai feels Esther should step up to the plate or "relief and deliverance for the Jews will arise from another place..." He may not have known how God will save his people, but he is confident that with or without Esther, it will happen.

Esther once approached the king when she heard of a plot for his murder. Now, it was time for her to save herself and her people. She could not keep silent. She loves her people. She loves her God.

The Beauty and Strength of Community

If Queen Esther and Mordecai were able to talk face-to-face, maybe he would have realized her deep concern. She had not forgotten who or whose she was. Her appointment to a royal position was not luck, fortune or chance. She begins to wonder if this was in God's plan from the very beginning. She's in the right place at the right time for the right reason and understands it's her time to step out on faith. Mordecai is right. "And who knows but that you have come to royal position for such a time as this?" Queen Esther is the star in God's plan to save His people.

At Queen Esther's request, Mordecai's next move is to gather all the Jews in Susa to fast for Esther over the next three days and three nights. They are to abstain from eating or drinking.

> ***In what ways have you experienced the beauty and strength of community, particularly in times of need?***

Her maids are not Jewish, but they too fast with her. They loved Esther and are concerned about her people. The Jews had initiated their own fast when they first heard about the edict calling for their lives. Now, the queen orders them to "fast for her." Esther needs the Jews to play an active role in calling on God for victory over their enemies. She knows the power of corporate prayer and fasting and the community admired her for being willing to give up her own life for the good of the whole.

The Role of Discernment

While neither Mordecai nor Esther mentioned God in this book of the Bible, their belief in Him is evident. Mordecai knows God is working behind the scenes. Esther knows her history and how God delivered the Israelites from Babylon. I tend to agree with scholars and others concerning Esther 4:14 as an indication of Mordecai's understanding of God's sovereignty. His will is being done. He is in control.

Queen Esther shows leadership at the point when she asked Mordecai to gather them to fast and pray. Throughout history, we see women called to lead in certain situations because they were needed to bring about change. Queen Esther became a situational leader faced with an enormous challenge.

When we seek God's help, He guides us, one step at a time. For most this is easier said than done, as we may want too much at once. When people are going through times of uncertainty or challenges about crucial decisions I always encourage them to stay in the moment to allow God's will to unfold.

It takes patience to wait on the Lord. Being still and quiet in His presence allows us to hear His will, His directions. Our desire should be to stay in step with the Spirit. The word gives us an image of what it is and is not in Psalm 32:9: *Do not be like the horse or the mule, which have no understanding but must be controlled by bit and bridle or they will not come to you.*

Keeping in step with the Spirit can be easy or it can be difficult. Are you anxious, discontent and hitting your head on closed doors? Narratives of those who followed the Lord are always excellent examples for learning this lesson.

When God gets us ready for a greater purpose, we don't necessarily know the fullness of His plan; however, by His grace, this is where our faith comes in.

I love to dance. In particular, I love to "social," which is what we called slow dance in the 70's. It is done on a large dance floor involving two people—a leader and a follower. It can't work when you have two leaders or two followers. Within a few minutes on the dance floor I can generally tell whether or not my partner is a good dancer. In many cases I could have easily taken the lead if my partner seemed unsure, but most of the time I "tried" to let him lead.

As a follower, you must trust the leader's body movements to guide you in making each step. The arms and legs have a key role. As a follower, you cannot move too fast or too slow. You have to keep in step with your leader because he knows where he wants to take you. Together, you enjoy the dance from the beginning to the end.

Dancing is one way of describing how God leads us and we follow. He knows the plan and the moves to get us from point A to point B. All we have to do is trust His lead. If we are too busy we cannot hear His voice or sense where the Spirit is leading. *His word is a lamp unto my feet and a light unto my path* (Psalm 119:105). We are to be like little children and allow our Father to lead because He knows how to connect the dots. He knows where He wants to take us. Once we become an adult, we may not want to think about being child-like. This does not please the Father. Learning how to listen, watch and pray with childlike wonder and faith, will lead us to the next step. After that initial step, we can trust God to lead us the rest of the way.

Esther wants to hear from God about her next step. She's willing to take risks. One lesson the Spirit has graciously taught me is not to be influenced by what other people think I should do, particularly if my best interest is not in mind. It's important to pray and seek God's will, even when listening to others. The Holy Spirit helps us to discern how to proceed and even uses others to be the voice of wisdom and confirmation. For Queen Esther, Mordecai became that voice of wisdom and confirmation.

Discernment is asking God to help us decide what to do based on His will, not ours. We should consider spiritual discernment as a daily practice in life, particularly when difficult decisions must be made. Author Richard J. Foster says in *Celebration of Discipline,* that we must put ourselves in a position to hear from God. If I am always busy, it might be hard to hear from Him. Sitting alone in quietness is a good posture to hear from God.

It is the awareness of His presence and activity in your life. Discernment is impossible without the work of the Holy Spirit: our Teacher, Counselor, Comforter and Enabler. Discernment is so critical that a leader without it is handicapped.

I remember being with a group of pastors in a leadership group with a regional pastor in our denomination. All three of us were seeking God about our next assignment. Our mentor said we needed discernment to know whether God is calling you to stay where you are, calling you to leave where you are into something else, or calling you to a place unknown. I was the last of those pastors to leave my assignment. I was being called out of my current assignment without knowing where I was going. I admit that I did wonder, "Why me?" Later, I thought, "Why not me?"

It took several years of struggle to find out that it was God's will for me to leave my role as pastor of the church even when I had no idea why or where I would go. In that, I found peace. This was one of the greatest acts of obedience and leaps of faith in my life. I found out that even then, God had a purpose in mind. We don't necessarily realize this until we obey.

God got me to the point of not playing "the victim," but to walk in the victory we have in Jesus Christ. One of my Facebook friends posted this quote by Mandy Hale, "Strong women don't play victim, don't make themselves look pitiful, & don't point fingers. They stand & they deal." The Holy Spirit teaches us to "stand and deal."

Leaving my role as pastor was not a decision made on my own because I thought it might be greener on the other side or that there was something wrong with the church—or me. I left because He released me and I obeyed.

I am careful not to look for signs or confirmations from others. Notice I said, "look." I know people who look for signs or words from God through other people. One woman I know kept asking me if I had a sign from God for her. I told her to stop looking. When we look for them, we find them, and they may not necessarily be from God. If it is God's will, He may give a sign in his timing not ours. In my experience, confirmation comes unexpectedly and mostly without a sense of urgency. Almost always, it comes in community.

For instance, I might have a conversation with someone pertaining to something totally different than what I am waiting to hear from God about. In that conversation, I sense a nudge or an impression from the Holy Spirit relating to something I am seeking God's will on. It stems from something said or observed unrelated to my concern.

It gets my attention. Amazingly, it ends in a sense of peace and clarity about what I am to do. I've also noticed that when people say you have to do this or do it now, my internal antenna goes up. Sometimes it is not as much about what is said versus how it is said.

I might struggle in discerning God's will sometimes. What is this about? It is like riding on a Merry-Go-Round that won't stop. My thoughts are constantly focused on a concern I am seeking Him about…up and down, round and round. I can't say this is the best use of my mind, but it happens. The problem is that my mind is on the concern and not on God.

When it comes to the point of focusing on God and not my circumstances, I might make a list of "pros" and "cons." I find it helpful in exploring the reality of a situation. This is a practical step in seeking God's will. It shouldn't stop there.

I always value the wisdom of close friends who have my best interest in mind, particularly those who knew me when I've gone through times of testing and it was clear God's hand was on me. They know me well.

There are times when I pray, fast and sit in silence before the Lord after reading the scriptures. I ask the Holy Spirit to help me see how God is leading me. I need His vision. I've even cried out to the Lord.

I write in my journal daily. I might record those things I know God told me to do; then I make a list of what He has not told me to do. I ask what doors are opening or closing? Who is in my life right now? What am I learning through these situations and people?

One morning during the week before going to the church I put on my walking shoes and left the house with the determination to keep walking until God spoke to my spirit about a certain situation. I got to the main road and kept straight as I listened to the many cars go by. I was prepared to walk until I dropped. I got a little more than a mile down the street and there was a Do Not Enter sign. I smiled, stopped, turned around and headed back toward home.

God knew there was a roadblock ahead. We often run into roadblocks and instead of going another way, we may just need to stop. We can want something so badly that nothing will stop us from getting it, not even a roadblock. We ignore the red flags. We try to walk around the barriers.

Discernment helps us to know when to pull back or proceed. On the other side of the Do Not Enter sign on my street, I noticed the roads were busted up because work was being done to repair the bridge on the other side. Continuing my walk could have been quite risky. The barriers were there for a good reason.

A few days later, I heard on the radio a warning asking people not to travel in that particular part of the city because it was dangerous. This was the same area I was walking toward on my walk to hear from God. I took this as a nudge from God that I should not enter this new situation I had been praying about. I was led to wait! God knows what's on the other side of our concerns and prayers and sees what lies ahead. He protects us from things unknown. Each one of us has to know His voice, how He speaks, teaches and leads us.

God spoke to me through this "sign" that I did not need to persist in the direction I wanted to go concerning a particular situation. Instead, I needed to wait on the Lord and I felt the peace of God in my heart.

I continue to learn how to be led by the Holy Spirit, walk by faith and leave the results to God. This is one of my deepest desires. It's a lifelong process to have the peace that surpasses all understanding and is the greatest determining factor in discerning God's will.

With that said, I've been tremendously blessed by the following words and have shared them with others during their own difficult times in life. In Thomas Merton's *The Road Ahead,* his prayer is, "My Lord God, I have no idea where I am going, I do not see the road ahead of me, I cannot know for certain where it will end. Nor do I really know myself, and the fact that I think I am following Your will does not mean that I am actually doing so. But I believe that the desire to please You does in fact please You. And I hope I have that desire in all that I am doing. I hope that I will never do anything apart from that desire. And I know that if I do this You will lead me by the right road, though I may know nothing about it. Therefore, I will trust You always, though I may seem to be lost and in the shadow of death. I will not fear, for You are ever with me, and You will never leave me to face my perils alone."

When Merton speaks of his desire to please God, this is that attitude of surrender. This is what we desire about all things. It isn't easy. It is a continuous learning process. We might revert to how we made decisions before we were concerned about seeking God's will, but we continue the journey of seeking His will. If what God is asking of us seems too costly, we might turn back out of fear. I believe this happens often because we are most comfortable in what we know instead of walking by faith.

A lot depends on where we are in our spiritual journey. We should all desire the point of surrender whereas we say like Jesus, "Not my will, but Your will be done." A price is paid to get to this point, but it is worth it. Nothing is greater than surrender to His will. Unfortunately, many abort and stand in a position of disobedience instead of going through. This is not unusual.

When we don't understand why God is requesting us to step out of our comfort zone, we have to learn how to trust Him anyway. We have to make time to know Him. *For My thoughts are not your thoughts, neither are your ways, My ways, declares the Lord. As the heavens are higher than the earth, so are My ways higher than your ways and My thoughts than your thoughts* (Isaiah 55:8-9). *The wise in heart are called discerning...* (Proverbs 16:27).

In the New Testament, we know what to ask for in James 5:1: *If any of you lacks wisdom, he should ask God, who gives generously to all without finding fault, and it will be given to him.* Wisdom from God gives us the capacity to do the right thing on our journey in life.

I also think of discernment as red, yellow and green lights. All three are equally important. When we encounter a red sign we should stop. This can be a real challenge when we desperately want something or we think someone is keeping us from having what God wants us to have. The more appealing something is, the more difficult it is to let it go. Under these circumstances, things do not quite add up. Things are not what they appear to be or maybe you are not the right person for a particular assignment. It's tough not to do something when everything in you wants to do it whether it is good or bad.

I admit that sometimes I might literally run a red light while driving. Given the choice of stopping abruptly or flying through when it's just about to turn red, sometimes I choose the latter. When it came to discerning what the right action in a given situation was, I recall not paying attention to the "lights." The consequences were costly, but it taught me obedience. Sometimes it takes a few or more mistakes before we learn a more excellent way. While in seminary, I was a resident assistant. I took pleasure in bringing or seeing that meals were taken to our sick hall mates, assuring the quiet hours were followed and

The Beauty and Strength of Community

making it a nice place to live together in community. I lived through a difficult moment when there was a lack of harmony on our floor relating to a dorm restriction. I took the advice of another woman about how to handle this situation.

My friend had a good plan but not the right plan. In my spirit I did not think it was the right thing to do. I didn't listen to that still soft voice. I messed up big time! Ignoring God's voice may come with consequences. It seemed like all hell broke loose. If it were not for another friend reaching out to me in this dark moment of my life, I feel like I would have perished. I, not speaking for anyone else, had to learn the hard way how to listen and obey God.

That lesson taught me the difference between His way, my way and anybody else's way. It was one, bright red light I should not have ignored. It got messy for a long period, but God assured me it would come to an end. It did.

The greatest lesson learned was to stop when something is not in agreement with your spirit. Be patient and keep seeking His will. God will work it out. With the Lord's help, I think I get it now. I know how important it is to take these matters to the Lord in prayer and then wait for His response. I know what it's like to wrestle until you have the answer. It is dangerous to step out on our own or do what other people suggest. The consequences can be devastating; but all is not lost. In Hebrews 12:11 it says, *No discipline is enjoyable while it is happening – it is painful! But afterward there will be a quiet harvest of right living for those who are trained in this way.* It's God's way of showing us just how much He loves us. I'm closer to right living today because of this one incident.

Consider a Greater Purpose
Vashti, Esther and the Courageous Women who Followed

One of the most costly lessons, I, and other women learn is in relationships. We become blinded by a strong desire to be involved with someone who may not be God's choice. What seems "good" is not necessarily "right" for you. This is when someone who loves us will try to help us see what we cannot see about a particular individual. Sometimes we become so wrapped up in a relationship that we wouldn't see any red lights if God literally flashed them right in front of our faces. All we think about is going to the chapel to get married. It is to our best interest not to ignore red lights!

A yellow sign means to yield, take it slow. Sometimes it means the timing is not right for us to continue in the same direction. Pause for further instructions. It was two years between the time I knew God was leading me to go to seminary and when I actually went. After it became clear to me that this was the direction God was leading me, I researched various seminaries to find the right one. I was sure Columbia International University was where God wanted me to go. This meant leaving Michigan to move to South Carolina.

I put my house on the market, but it did not sell. The market was sluggish at the time. I talked to my pastor and he advised me to wait on the Lord. Perhaps it was not time. I maintained my job and waited on the Lord. One night while lying in bed I felt a gentle nudge. I interpreted it as, "it was now time to go to seminary."

In a response to what I perceived as being obedient to God, I asked for three things regarding the sale of my house: 1) it would sell in one week; 2) it would sell with a conventional mortgage and 3) it would sell at the current market price. All three happened. God's will was clear.

How many times should you have waited a little longer? I do not know where this originated, but someone said, "God's delay is not His denial."

I think we like green lights the most. A green light means to go—don't linger, just go! This was real in my own life. When I learned about a co-pastor opening at Immanuel Christian Reformed Church, I fasted and prayed for forty days to discern God's will before making the move back to Michigan. It certainly wasn't easy. On the thirty-seventh day I thought I would be sick.

When I left Detroit four years earlier, I never thought I would live in Michigan again. I inquired about the Christian Reformed denomination with one of the professors and got the okay to pursue it. I did further research in the library. After it was clear that I was to accept this new position, I received a word of knowledge from a staff person that in this new position, I would be like Daniel in the den of lions. Wow! I understood and nodded my head. I was grateful for her obedience to what the Holy Spirit had put in her spirit. So many times after this word was spoken to me, I read Daniel's story.

While the Jews were in captivity in Babylon, Daniel, who was a Jew with "exceptional qualities," had been identified by King Darius to eventually become the governor over the whole kingdom. This did not set well with some evil administrators. They wanted to trap Daniel into doing something wrong to keep him from being exalted. They convinced King Darius to issue a decree that no one should pray to another god or man other than the king during a thirty-day period. They knew Daniel was a praying man. However, although Daniel knew about the decree, he did not stop getting on his knees to pray three times a day upstairs in an opened window in his house facing Jerusalem. Daniel did exactly what his enemies hoped he would do and they caught him praying to God. The king was very disturbed that he had to go through with sending Daniel into the den of lions.

But, even with the stone placed and sealed over the opening of the den, the lions did not devour Daniel. The Lord kept him and Daniel wasn't afraid of the lions. We see the importance of God in Daniel's life and how he knew his help would come from the Lord. Daniel's life was spared because God sent an angel to shut the mouths of the lions. Daniel was innocent in the eyes of God of any wrongdoings so God protected him for a greater message to be sent to his persecutors and the king.

When Daniel emerged from the den unharmed the king was in total shock. God allowed Daniel to be placed in the den of lions. Why? We do not know. Many times God's reasons are unknown to us and beyond our understanding. When we faithfully serve and obey God, however, He will always be right there with us no matter where we are.

God led me to Kalamazoo, Michigan, to serve at Immanuel Christian Reformed Church. He gave me the green light; therefore, I knew I was going to be just fine. As was shared with me before I took the position, the ministry was difficult, but it was filled with many blessings. A green light does not mean life is going to be easy. It means this is God's will for you. It is not unusual for Him to use these Daniel-like experiences to shape us for a greater purpose.

As I have experienced going to God in situations, I can imagine Esther's struggle with the decision to approach the king. What if she really wasn't ready to give up all the royalty? If we are honest with ourselves—which is not always easy—we don't know what we would have done if we were in Queen Esther's shoes.

At Immanuel, the temptation to dismiss the message given to me about Daniel in the den of lions and to leave when the going got tough became a challenge; but I never forgot the lion's den analogy. God had a greater purpose and I needed to always consider that. We don't necessarily believe when we're having difficulty in a situation that it comes from God. Instead of trusting God and walking by faith, we lean on our own understanding, give into fear or seek an easier assignment. Each becomes distractions or deterrents. The truth is that God cares about us, and He wants us to be fully alive to His will.

10 Considerations for Discerning God's Will

1) Alignment with your values, talents, spiritual gifts and strengths;

2) Right connections – God connects you with people and resources to help you accomplish His will;

3) Significant milestones of your journey leading to this new assignment;

4) Doors open and doors close – don't force it;

5) Sense of peace;

6) Awareness of need to trust God;

7) Affirmation and/or confirmation from others in the Body of Christ;

8) Time set aside for fasting and prayer (maybe ask others to join you);

9) Awareness of spiritual warfare and standing against evil forces;

10) Presence of God – recognizing you're involved in something bigger than yourself!

The Decision

Queen Esther's decision to approach the king is made in community. She yielded (fasting and praying) and then moved forward with the confidence that she was in sync with God. There was only one obstacle... approaching the king.

Mordecai's words kept ringing in her head, that God brought her to the kingdom for "such a time as this." She trusted the fasting done by the people, servants and herself. The strength she received from the Heavenly Father led to her confidence to approach her earthly king.

> **With great enthusiasm the Esther reading group interpreted "If I perish, I perish!" as "Let's roll, I'll do it!"**

She contemplated the consequences. She thought of Vashti and the lengthy, yet conceivable process of finding a new queen. Being selected over so many was an honor. But, this wasn't about her. Head held high in confidence she understood, "And, if I perish, I perish."

From the beginning, we have seen a young woman who knows God's loving-kindness and tender mercies. She believes the same God who brought her ancestors out of slavery in Egypt and delivered them from Babylonian captivity would save His chosen people. Esther's love of God shines through in her surrender to His will. He is the same God who took care of her when she was left as an orphan. Esther continues to think about the fingerprints of God in her life.

We often forget to pause when we have difficult decisions to make to see where God is already working. An element of trust on our part is because typically we are being asked by God to do something greater than anything we have done before.

Her heart is set on pleasing God. *If the Lord delights in a man's way, He makes his steps firm; though he stumble, he will not fall, for the Lord upholds him with His hand,* (Psalm 37:23- 24).

God's people have hope. The mothers who pray for their children are not without hope. Some mothers would even give their lives in order to save a dying child.

Esther is a yielded vessel. She, too, vowed to risk her life to save her people. She may have prayed something like this:

Keep me safe, my God, for in You, I take refuge.

I say to the Lord, "You are my Lord; apart from You I have no good thing." I say of the holy people who are in the land, "They are the noble ones in whom is all my delight.

Lord, You alone are my portion and my cup; You make my lot secure. The boundary lines have fallen for me in pleasant places; surely I have a delightful inheritance. I will praise the Lord, who counsels me; even at night my heart instructs me. I keep my eyes always on the Lord. With Him at my right hand, I will not be shaken.

*Therefore my heart is glad and my tongue rejoices; my body also will rest secure, because You will not abandon me to the realm of the dead, nor will You let your faithful one see decay. You make known to me the path of life; You will fill me with joy in Your presence, with eternal pleasures at Your right hand (*Psalm 16:1-3, 5-11) (capital You, added by author for emphasis).

She calls on the God plenteous in mercy who, bows down to those who come earnestly to His throne of grace. She lifts up her soul to the Sovereign God. She approaches a forgiving and good God who abounds in love to all who call on His name. Again she asks God to hear her prayer and listen to her cry for mercy.

Esther knows how much He delights in those who call on His name. She knows that all other gods are absolutely nothing in comparison to *Adonai (*Lord). She trusts in Him because He is faithful. She knows that joy comes not from the king's abundance, but from God. He is great and His works are marvelous. He alone is God. She knows life is worth living only when she walks in His truth; therefore, she stresses the importance of being taught by God. Living without His teaching means she walks in darkness and not in the light of His presence.

Leading without His guidance is not an option. Esther desires complete loyalty to the King of Kings and Lord of Lords. She rests in God's infinite mercy in dealing with the Jews' ruthless enemy, Haman. What a beautiful image of God bowing down to show mercy to His children in the midst of their troubles. He's not so high that He can't reach down and save us from any schemes of the devil.

She is asking for divine protection for her life and the life of the Jews. She prays for favor with King Xerxes. As much as she loves the king, there is no one like the Lord—compassionate and gracious, slow to anger, abounding in love and faithfulness. She will break out in praise with all her heart, which gains His attention, as she gives God all the glory He desires and deserves.

Some believe that the book of Esther would have been a love story had Haman and his vain destruction not turned it into a drama. However, God still has the leading role and He demonstrated His love for His people by sacrificing His one and only Son. Esther demonstrates love for her people by the willingness to sacrifice her own life. She is leading the way as a role model of courage.

Knowing God has called her for such a time as this perhaps causes Esther to ask for what she no doubt needs—His favor. He is the only one who can bring victory! Could Esther have prayed and prayed all day long like Hannah prayed for God to give her a son? Did she pray for a sign of His goodness? "Lord, just show my enemies that you are working it out."

Against all odds, God's help and comfort will cause Esther to stand firm in the trying of her faith. She knows that He will make her way straight. He promises to make our way straight. *Trust in the Lord with all your heart and lean not on your own*

The Beauty and Strength of Community

understanding; in all your ways acknowledge Him, and He will make your paths straight (Proverbs 3:5-6).

My desire is "Lord, make my way straight so that I may follow You every step of the way no matter how difficult life might be." I've been blessed by Psalm 138:3, *When I called, You answered me; You greatly emboldened me.*

That strength comes from God and community. Such a time came one day while I was at work. I had an important assignment to lead a group, and I was anxious. I didn't know if I would be successful so I prayed Psalm 138:3.

To relax, I scheduled an appointment for a massage—yes, in the middle of the day. Afterwards, I realized just how good I felt. The tension in my shoulders was gone. While setting up for the meeting, a peer came into the room. She thought she was late, however there was almost a whole hour before the meeting was to begin. I asked if she would stay and pray with me. I had known her to be a praying woman and I would have been surprised if she said no. We prayed together for nearly thirty minutes. I felt the peace of God come upon me and in the atmosphere, proving once again that the Lord answers our prayers.

The event was beyond what I, and perhaps others, had anticipated. God used the massage and my peer to give me the strength needed both physically and spiritually. What initially caused me stress and anxiety became a blessing.

I've said it to others and it has been said to me, "You're called for such a time as this." This statement, oftentimes, is right on target and conveys that the person receiving it is about to do something that is greater than them.

On the night of September 25, 2012, I was coming to the end of my third month after leaving the pastorate. I was doing my evening routine of reading before bed and was finishing up *Soul Searching:* The Journey of Thomas Merton. I placed many pillows in the bed around me so that I was quite comfortable.

In the midst of reading I closed my eyes to meditate on the words, "God alone." These two words were carved over the doors of the monastery where Merton lived. For him, he needed to be cleansed from the false romanticism of being a monk and leaving an evil world. It was not until then would he bear much fruit and realize the beauty of a social life.

That night, I had my "God alone" experience. The next thing that happened was unexpected. I became so restless as seen by my hands moving as if they had been bound, and my legs and feet moving as if chains were holding them down. I encountered a struggle, an inner conflict between the flesh and the spirit.

In Galatians 5:16-18, it speaks of this conflict. Although I cannot necessarily name those things in my life, which were holding me back from entering a deeper attitude of surrender to God, I experienced a strong sense of release. Symbolically, the wrestling was necessary in order for those shackles and chains to come off—a deeper attitude of surrender. He wants an undivided, clean heart. Merton's struggle was for a different reason than mine, but both would lead to bearing more fruit and preparation for a greater purpose—surely something beyond my imagination. I pray I am open to whatever God wants to accomplish through my life.

Reflections

1. Queen Esther had the support of the Jewish community and those closest to her in discerning God's will. How likely are you to seek the support of the broader community to join you in praying and/or fasting concerning a challenging situation?

2. Tell of a time when you experienced the beauty and strength of community.

3. In what ways might you set aside time to seek God's face in difficult situations?

4. What did the statement, "And if I perish, I perish," mean for Queen Esther?

5. What does this statement mean for you?

Prayer

Father, when I find myself particularly in situations that seem so impossible, I pray that I will turn to You for help and wisdom to do what is pleasing in Your eyes. I will not turn my back and ignore difficult situations. I look to You, Lord! I will seek others to stand in the gap with me in fasting and prayer, if necessary. Above all, I know that Jesus Christ, our Intercessor, is sitting on the right hand of Your throne pleading on my behalf. You, O Lord, will hear and answer me when I call. Thank You. It's in the name of Jesus I pray. AMEN.

Notes

When he saw Queen Esther standing in the court, he was pleased with her and held out to her the gold scepter that was in his hand. So Esther approached and touched the tip of the scepter. Then the king asked, "What is it, Queen Esther? What is your request? Even up to half the kingdom, it will be given you.

Esther 5:2-3

"My hope,…is that through children, they will begin to educate their families and that will, in turn, begin to educate our communities. [I'm] using this platform to help change lives. We have to be healthy."

First Lady Michelle Obama

Words spoken shortly after the unveiling of the Presidential Garden on the grounds of the White House she planted along with elementary school children from the Washington D.C. area.

Chapter 8
Extending the Gold Scepter

Consider a Greater Purpose
Vashti, Esther and the Courageous Women who Followed

A Platform Makes a Difference

Queen Esther was in a position to save her people. She was not that powerless young lady who first came to the harem without a clue of what she would encounter in the royal palace. God elevated Esther. She was in a position of influence with knowledge of how she could save her people from the hands of an evil man. However, she did not know if the king would extend his scepter to her in an invitation for a platform to influence.

We celebrate the work of all women who understand how to use a platform to make a difference. Having a platform to influence is a gift. Sometimes it comes with a particular position or role in an organization. Other times it is a platform inherited by a family legacy or out of a personal passion to promote a need or a cause.

Each day we see politicians, authors, actresses, teachers, physicians, parents, children, clergy, former addicts, entertainers and others who dedicate themselves to making a positive change in their community, country and/or the world. Each generation makes their own contribution in positively influencing the lives of others.

First Lady Michelle Obama is an example of a woman who saw a platform as a catalyst for changing lives. Being very aware of the major diseases that plague our society—particularly young children—she decided to do something about it. The vegetables and fruits grown in the public garden on the grounds of the White House were also used for cooking meals for the First Family.

Extending the Gold Scepter

Children came to put their hands in the soil, cultivate the soil, plant seeds and later to enjoy the harvest. Michelle's vision is healthier people. She joined others in elevating this cause that will have lasting effects even after her family leaves the White House. The focus on the health of children was given an even larger stage when Michelle—The First Lady—endorsed the efforts in collaboration with other health organizations giving it the attention it deserved. While being First Lady carries a lot of weight when it comes to people supporting a cause she endorses, those in the media also have great influence over public opinion and actions.

Robin Roberts, broadcast journalist and co-host of *Good Morning America*, says she was inspired by tennis great Arthur Ashe. In her early years, Robin played for and led the Southeastern Louisiana Women's Basketball team, and later anchored ESPN's SportsCenter and NFL Primetime. A door opened for her to become the first woman to host an NFL pre-game show. She touched many lives with her beautiful smile, transparency and resilience.

In 2005, she was asked to leave her job in sports news casting to become a co-anchor on the *Good Morning America* talk show. She wrestled with the decision of leaving an arena where women were rarely represented, feeling she would disappoint young women who looked up to her as a role model.

It was not until Robin mentioned this concern to Billie Jean King, a former tennis pro, that her eyes were opened to accept a bigger platform. Without beating around the bush, King said, "Robin, snap out of it. You'll take all of us with you, and when you do talk about women in sports, you'll have a bigger platform." This is exactly what Robin needed to hear. She took the job on *Good Morning America* where she won the hearts of those who not only respected her as a sports journalist, but those who learned of her for the first time as a morning host.

Years after taking on the show, Robin was diagnosed with cancer. Her battle with the disease in 2007 and again in 2012 gained a national audience. As she struggled to be strong for her viewers, she became a powerful voice for surviving cancer. Through the lens of the camera, viewers were able to follow her to her appointments with radiation treatments, chemotherapy and a bone marrow transplant.

Many of us viewers prayed with Robin, her mother and siblings as they fought through it together. The illness of cancer couldn't compare to the loss of Robin's mother just before her transplant. Her courage was commended. She inspired so many. In 2013, she was the recipient of the Arthur Ashe Courage Award, which is awarded to those who excel in sports.

As you think about your own life, perhaps doors have opened for you to exceed your own expectations. I've found myself on platforms I never thought or dreamed of. I've learned when my focus is on God's desire to use me to make change it becomes less about my personal desires for my life.

God's thoughts and ways are far greater than ours and we may not ever know the fullness of what He has done through us to bring change and transformation in the lives of others. I thank Him for every platform given to influence others. The key is to

Extending the Gold Scepter

understand the extent to which you can use a platform, and then proceed as the Spirit leads.

Permission to Approach the King

Esther steps out in faith as she makes her request to see the king. It had been three days of fasting and now was the moment she had been waiting for. Wearing a royal robe she stands in the inner court of the palace looking stunning. As the king spots her from his royal throne he marvels at her beauty.

It has been thirty days since he last summoned her to his presence. Their eyes meet as he lifts the gold scepter and extends it toward her. She graciously moves forward, touching the tip of the scepter. She now has the access she had been praying for.

The words Esther is hoping to hear from the king are spoken: "What is it, Queen Esther? What is your request? Even up to half the kingdom, it will be given you." He is generous and willing to give her half of the kingdom.

> ***How sensitive are you to recognizing "gateways" to expressing your deepest needs?***

Consider a Greater Purpose
Vashti, Esther and the Courageous Women who Followed

To have access is powerful and liberating. Sometimes, it only comes through invitation. Although Queen Esther takes the initial step in approaching the king, there is more. What happens next is similar to the scene in the book of Nehemiah. When King Artaxerxes notices the sadness of his cupbearer, Nehemiah, he asks why he is sad. Nehemiah shares with the king his desire to rebuild the wall. The king provides him with an abundance of resources—financial and manpower—to bring the desire to fruition.

Expressing Your Needs

In my generation (Baby Boomers) some of us were taught to graciously accept what is given to us without expressing our desires or needs for something else. In some ways being thankful for what you have in order to not be perceived as ungrateful. Subsequently, our true needs may have been unexpressed or suppressed.

This teaching led me to allow others to make decisions for me without any concern for my thoughts or feelings. Could a sense of not being worthy or having something important to say contribute to this? Could an attitude that "it won't make any difference what I say" be destructive? Paying attention to destructive patterns needs to be considered. Fear or any other reason should not be a factor that keeps us from asking for what we need, even if it is asked for others.

Let me make it plain. I often see this pattern with couples. Maybe the woman is upset, coldhearted or nonresponsive to her partner. He asks, "What's wrong?" extending the "gold scepter." She says, "Nothing." Her needs are stored away instead of being met. Her partner never learns what she really needs from him. This is a destructive pattern affecting generation after generation of couples. One day my leadership coach asked if I needed anything. Wow! I rarely think about what I need. I paused. This was my homework. Write down what you need to be effective at <u>fill in the blank.</u>

I completed my assignment. I discovered that, 1) I have needs; 2) it's okay to have needs; and 3) it's okay to let others know of my needs. Lesson: When the "scepter" is extended, use the opportunity to express yourself and what you truly need or desire.

Subsequent to this session with my leadership coach, I became intentional in articulating my needs when asked or when it was appropriate to speak up. It feels good! I was released from the bondage. Will you recognize when the "gold scepter" is being extended to you?

One thing I have noticed in my newfound freedom to express my needs, is the importance of seizing the moment. I had a situation in which I felt like my performance evaluation did not reflect what I had contributed to an organization. I have no problems sleeping, but that night I didn't sleep well. The next morning while having my devotion, I prayed for an opportunity to have a conversation about the evaluation. God answered my prayer and gave me the courage I needed.

Just like any other morning, my supervisor and I greeted one another. I asked for an opportunity to talk; it happened so smoothly. Shortly afterwards, the "gold scepter" was extended. We scheduled a meeting and discussed my concerns. To my surprise we had similar thoughts about the evaluation and through the grace of God it was changed in my favor.

Some desires for the scepter (access) are not as easy to have as others. An example of this is when I wanted to attend a Pastors' Fellowship Breakfast in Detroit at a local church. Dr. Tony Evans, Pastor of Oak Cliff Bible Fellowship and President of The Urban Alternative, was guest speaker. I knew my pastor would not be attending so I called the church where the event would be held, to express my desire to attend this event.

I was told that my name would be placed on the list and someone would give me a call. Well, I waited…and waited for weeks. I called again. This time I learned that my gender was an issue. At the time, I was not a clergy, but I was very woman!

A couple weeks later a close friend called to ask if I would be willing to go to the Detroit Metropolitan Airport to pick up Mrs. Lois Evans, Dr. Evans' wife. I didn't know at the time that my friend was on the event planning committee. Of course, I agreed! It was a very pleasant ride and Mrs. Evans' beauty radiates from the inside out.

She asked me several questions about myself. After years of working for a major computer company, I was waiting on God to show me the next phase of my life. She asked about my future plans…she extended the scepter. It was never my intent to tell Mrs. Evans about the situation concerning the Pastors Fellowship Breakfast, but I did. I honored the opportunity.

Mrs. Evans became very concerned when she heard of my dilemma of not being allowed to attend the event because I was a woman. I dropped her off at the hotel and she promised to see if Dr. Evans would approve of my attendance. About an hour later she called, as she said she would, with the message that: "Dr. Evans would love for you to join us."

At the event, only two women in attendance—Lois and myself. I never could have attended that event without her help. Dr. Evans gave me access that I couldn't gain on my own. It was a divine connection.

Praise the Lord! Oh, what a fellowship, what a joy divine! Without God this would not have been possible.

Now that Esther was in, she had to play it safe. She wants to tell the king about Haman's role in this evil attack against the Jewish people of his provinces. But, she waited and listened for the right time.

She anticipated the king asking her what she needed. She thinks. She is ready to answer the king's question, "What do you want?" She tells him of her desire to invite the king and Haman for a special banquet.

The Esther reading group response:

Queen Esther has a strategy. Having a strategy for a life-changing conversation is a good idea. She knew the situation was bigger than her.

Reflections

1. What platforms of influence are you privileged to? How are you making a difference in using that influence?

2. What situation calls for someone of power and authority to extend the "gold scepter" in order for you to move forward in "being" or "doing" something you are passionate about?

3. Is there someone who needs you to extend the gold scepter to her/him because you have access to something she/he needs?

4. Talk about how Esther handled her situation. What do you like or dislike about what she did?

5. What does this chapter say to you about God, yourself and others?

Prayer

Gracious and loving Father, hear my prayer. Give me the courage to stand up for what is right in Your eyes and to speak boldly for those who do not have the same privileges that I have. Whether it is in a gentle or strong voice, give me the words to say what needs to be said in the right moment. Give me the desire to move from words to action to promote whatever work You call me to. Just as you extended the gold scepter to be part of Your Kingdom, I will tell others of Your grace and mercy. In the name of Jesus. Amen.

Notes

"Bring Haman at once," the king said, "so that we may do what Esther asks."

So the king and Haman went to the banquet Esther had prepared. As they were drinking wine, the king again asked Esther, "Now what is your petition? It will be given you. And what is your request? Even up to half the kingdom, it will be granted."

Esther replied, "My petition and my request is this: If the king regards me with favor and if it pleases the king to grant my petition and fulfill my request, let the king and Haman come tomorrow to the banquet I will prepare for them. Then I will answer the king's question."

Esther 5:5-8

"I shall not march at all unless I can march under the Illinois banner."

Ida B. Wells-Barnett

Advocate of civil, women and economic rights

(July 15, 1862 – March 25, 1931)

Chapter 9
Setting the Stage

It's a Set Up

Esther's setting the stage to present her request to the king. After one banquet, she took a chance of taking two days from the king's schedule for another feast where she will tell him what she desires. Haman's chest sticks out at the thought of being the only person invited to dine with the king and queen. Quite naturally, he is honored.

In the meantime, outside of the palace at the king's gate, Haman sees his worst enemy, Mordecai. It bothers him that Mordecai simply ignores him. Haman can't stomach Mordecai's fearlessness and the fact that he is not afraid to stand up for what he believes in—especially when it means disobeying orders to bow.

He will deal with Mordecai another time; for now he had to celebrate the fact that he had another invitation-only event to attend an exclusive banquet with the king and queen. He couldn't wait to get home to tell his wife, Zeresh, about it.

In the Esther reading group, Haman's overuse of "I" was noted. It is a sign of pride. However, he would be stopped! Even in light of the banquet invitation, Haman had a bad taste in his mouth when he thought of Mordecai. Let me just say it... Haman was evil!

The story has a battle between good and evil. Zeresh and friends come up with a conceivable solution to Haman's problem:

Setting the Stage

With the king's permission and before the party begins, hang Mordecai on a handmade 75-foot-high gallows. Haman liked this suggestion and proceeded in having the gallows built. Without Mordecai, his future holds a life of ease to eat, drink and be merry.

But, let's not get ahead of ourselves.

When Haman decided to kill Mordecai and all the Jews, he cast the lot to select the day and month to kill them. He didn't get the king's permission for those details. Now, again without getting the king's approval, he is having the gallows built to kill Mordecai that next day. There's no respect and loyalty to the king.

*Haman is a powerful man. (*As far as the king is concerned, Haman is "all that and a bag of chips" as said by the Esther reading group.*) As he sleeps, he probably dreams of the banquet. For the king, it was a different story.*

Uneasiness comes over the king and keeps him from falling asleep. He ordered his attendant to read the records of his reign to him—always a good bedtime story. As his attendant read, he gets to the part of record when Mordecai exposes the king's two officers, Bigthana and Teresh, in a plot to kill him. Xerxes notices that there was nothing written about the honor or recognition given to Mordecai for his act of loyalty to the king.

Out of curiosity, he asks the attendant about this, who confirms no recognition had been given for this life-saving action. When Haman arrives in the court the king asks, "Who is in the court?"

Consider a Greater Purpose
Vashti, Esther and the Courageous Women who Followed

The king thwarted Haman's plan to tell him about the gallows he built to hang Mordecai. The king wants to know how to honor a man who pleases the king. Haman feels pretty good about himself. Why wouldn't he? The queen did invite him to dinner, twice!

> **Evidence of God's providence - The king cannot sleep and he asks his attendant to read the record of his reign to him.**

Haman imagines himself wearing a royal robe while riding on a horse that the king once rode. He sees himself being led through the city streets being proclaimed as the man the king delights to honor!

> **Evidence of God's providence - Haman arrives in the court and the king asks, "Who is in the court?" It's a set up! This is one of the moments I would love to be a fly on the wall to see Haman's face!**

Haman does everything in his power to keep his composure before the king as he makes suggestions on how to give honor in a royal way. The king loves the idea and orders Haman to immediately go, do these things—for Mordecai! Instead of Haman receiving the king's Man of the Year Award, it is earmarked for the man he hates. This was the highest mark of honor given to a subject by the king.

It took everything in Haman to robe Mordecai and lead him through the city streets as he heralded, "This is what is done for the man the king delights to honor!" Afterward, Mordecai returns to the king's gate, possibly to connect with Esther's maids to share the good news. Haman is totally humiliated and rushes home with the bad news to tell his wife, Zeresh, and his advisors. They are baffled. Then they make an observation about the Jews.

"Since Mordecai, before whom your downfall has started, is of Jewish origin, you cannot stand against him—you will surely come to ruin!" Things had not turned out the way they thought in the plot against Mordecai and they felt he may as well just stop trying to persecute him. But, Haman's pride continues to get in the way. This is not over. For now, the king's eunuchs have come to take him to the banquet.

The Time is Right

Haman made the assumption that he was to be honored by the king. Assumptions are hard to deal with when the person making the assumption is dead wrong. The repercussions of wrong assumptions fell on some delegates sent from Illinois to Washington, D.C., at the turn of the 20th Century. They assumed Ida B. Wells-Barnett, an advocate for civil, women and economic rights, would take their advice and march in the National American Woman Suffrage Association's suffrage parade with the Colored delegates in the rear of the lineup.

Marching in the rear would mean she could not represent her state of Illinois. They were dead wrong! Ida perceived this parade as an historical moment and she was not willing to be treated unfairly. She stood her ground arguing that "the southern women have tried to evade the question time and again by giving some excuse or other every time it has been brought up. If the Illinois women do not take a stand now in this great democratic parade, then the Colored women are lost."

The Illinois delegates would not listen to Ida or the Caucasians who stood with her. When some of the delegates did not see Ida later on, they assumed she had taken "her place" in the rear of the parade. It wasn't until the parade worked its way down Pennsylvania Avenue in the nation's Capitol that she took what she felt was her rightful place in line with the Illinois delegates.

This bold move led to her standing up for herself and other Colored women as she single-handedly integrated the parade, and the suffrage movement. It was the right time! Of all the things this newspaper editor did in her lifetime to stand up for the rights of African Americans this is one of Ida's most significant accomplishments.

Meanwhile, back at the palace...

The degradation Haman had felt earlier as he marched Mordecai into the streets in a hero's parade was still bitter on

Setting the Stage

his tongue. As he sat to sup with the royal family he assumed his exclusive invite was because he was such an amazing leader. The food was amazing and the wine was top notch. But, the king was still curious.

"Queen Esther, what is your petition?" the king asks. Haman too is anxiously waiting for an answer he will hear before anyone else in the palace. He and the king await the response with baited breath. She knows that what she says will change her life, for better or worse. But, the lives of her people are at stake. She takes a deep breath.

"If I have found favor with you, Your Majesty, and if it pleases you, grant me my life—this is my petition." The king is awestruck. What is going on? Her life? Is someone threatening her life? The king listens intensely. She is passionate and serious. She is not afraid, but respectful. She is not pushy, but direct. She is courageous with grace, wisdom and strength from God. The king has no idea what she is talking about.

She continues with an added plea to not only save her, but her people. Haman is trying to make sense of what she is saying. He has a plan to kill the Jews, not Queen Esther. King Xerxes and Haman are shocked—both for different reasons. Only the queen and Haman know the real deal. The king is still in a fog—who are her people?

Esther keeps her cool and goes into the details of how major genocide is being planned against her people, not slavery, but death. King Xerxes listens as his fury elevates.

Consider a Greater Purpose
Vashti, Esther and the Courageous Women who Followed

"Who is he? Where is he—the man who has dared to do such a thing?" Like a witness in a courtroom identifying the accused, Esther identifies Haman as the culprit. The king was so upset he stormed out and rushed into the palace garden. Haman was terrified. The king has not said anything to him, but he could see the look of anger on his face. Was he headed out to call the guards? Would he get a weapon and kill Haman himself?

Haman's life hangs in the balance as he and Esther are left alone. He takes this as an opportunity to plead for his life. He hurriedly falls onto the couch where the queen was reclining. He desperately grabs onto her, pleading for mercy.

As if the king weren't mad enough, he comes back into the banquet area to find Haman appearing to be molesting the queen. That's it! Without calling on his royal advisors or asking Haman his side of the story, the king sentences Haman to death. The eunuch, Harbona (one of the seven eunuchs sent to bring Queen Vashti to the king back in the beginning of the book of Esther) comes with a solution for how the king should have Haman killed. The king agrees with the plan to hang Haman on the same 75-foot high gallows he made for Mordecai.

> **The Esther reading group response:**
>
> **Haman did what so many people do even today; he did not consider the consequences of his actions.**

Setting the Stage

Protection from Evil

Psalm 141:9-10 says, *Keep me from the snares they have laid for me, from the traps set by evildoers. Let the wicked fall into their own nets, while I pass by in safety.* Haman fell into his own net. As he ate dinner with the queen, his wife, Zeresh, couldn't wait for him to come back and share the details of this second banquet. Instead, she would hear of the plan to hang her husband on the same gallows he had built for his enemy, Mordecai.

The reality of hatred and bitterness in the world is seen through the character of Haman who has hatred for others due to their religion, race, social status, etc. Haman may not have been such a bad guy had power and status not led to his destruction. This is a prime example of how pride comes before a fall.

The reality of pride comes before a fall is not only true in biblical days but throughout history and today. One of my neighbors was a member of the Esther reading group and was still excited about the opportunity to share the story together with other women. She mentioned how the discussion about Haman made her realize just how much Haman is in all of us. In fact, other women continued to email or call me about the impact the session had on them as it allowed them to take what was said about the characters and relate it to themselves or those in their own lives.

Even in my devotional time the week before talking to her, I was reminded that actions that do not bring honor to God can be deeply rooted in our heart. We need the Holy Spirit to help us search our heart for anything that does not align with the character of Jesus Christ. We know the repercussions of pride as we see it in others; however, we fail to see glimpses of it in ourselves.

Acknowledging our own brokenness and the holiness of God, should humble us in His presence. *He mocks proud mockers but gives grace to the humble (*Proverbs 3:34). Humility is something we all have to desire, receive from God and work on cultivating. It is pride that causes us to justify wrong and dismiss what is right.

C.S. Lewis' *Mere Christianity* teaches us how pride and being in the presence of God works when he says, "Whenever we find that our religious life is making us feel that we are good—above all, that we are better than someone else—I think we may be sure that we are being acted on, not by God, but by the devil. The real test of being in the presence of God is that you either forget about yourself altogether or see yourself as a small, dirty object."

We should daily strive to not put ourselves above others or to think we are incapable of having evil thoughts. We need God's grace to keep us humble and we can ask for it. When I am aware of thinking evil thoughts, I cast them down and replace them with God's truth because the truth will set you free. It takes prayer and discipline to keep from going down this trail.

In Jesus' Priestly Prayer in John 17:15 He says, *My prayer is not that you take them out of the world but that you protect them from the evil one.* Can we take this too lightly? Yes, we can! We don't want to fall into the hands of an evil person; nor do we want to put ourselves above others, like Haman, or to minister from an exalted instead of a humble position. There is no sense of Esther putting herself above Haman, but she was advocating for justice!

Lord, have mercy.

Reflections

1. What in this chapter surprises you?

2. What keeps you from seeking revenge from those who wrong you?

3. What are some practical ways to deal with evil?

4. In what ways does God remind you to deal with pride?

5. What does this chapter teach you about God, about yourself and about others?

Prayer
Almighty God, Creator and Sustainer of all things, thank You for Your faithfulness. You remind us over and over again that You are always present, even in the midst of our trials, struggles and suffering. You are always working all things for our good whether we see You or not. In time, we will understand all things. Lead us not into temptation but deliver us from all evil. We exalt Your name above all names. You are holy and righteous and worthy of all praise. In the name of Jesus we give You honor and praise. AMEN.

Notes

Esther again pleaded with the king, falling at his feet and weeping. She begged him to put an end to the evil plan of Haman the Agagite, which he had devised against the Jews. Then the king extended the gold scepter to Esther and she arose and stood before him.

"If it pleases the king," she said, "and if he regards me with favor and thinks it the right thing to do, and if he is pleased with me, let an order be written overruling the dispatches that Haman son of Hammedatha, the Agagite, devised and wrote to destroy the Jews in all the king's provinces. For how can I bear to see disaster fall on my people? How can I bear to see the destruction of my family?"

Esther 8:3-6

Blessed is she who has believed that the Lord would fulfill His promises to her!
And Mary said:
"My soul glorifies the Lord
and my spirit rejoices in God my Savior,
for He has been mindful of the humble state
of His servant.
From now on all generations will call me blessed,
for the Mighty One has done great things
for me—holy is His name.
His mercy extends to those who fear Him,
from generation to generation.

Luke 1:45-50

Mary, the mother of our Lord and Savior Jesus Christ

Chapter 10
Accomplishing God's Mission

Our Help Comes from the Lord

One of the most notable actions following Haman's death is Mordecai coming into the presence of the king after Esther reveals her secret identity as a Jew. The barrier between the king and Mordecai is removed as the king showers Mordecai with blessings.

First, the king gives Mordecai his signet ring, which was taken from Haman. Then Esther appoints him over all Haman's property, which is now hers. Mordecai would never forget what God had done by saving His people through Esther.

> *The Esther reading group response:*
>
> *In the book of Esther, the end of chapter 8 mirrors the beginning of chapter 1. What do you think?*

When we know our help comes from the Lord it makes this part of the story of Esther easy to understand and embrace. God removed barriers and only He could change their situation. Mordecai didn't intentionally create a barrier between he and Haman and he couldn't break it down. God is the Giver of all blessings, and positions us where we need to be "for such a time as this." We have to wait on Him and not lose hope when things don't seem to change. His timing is perfect and worth waiting for.

Accomplishing God's Mission

The Story is not Over Yet!

Though it seems Esther and Mordecai will live happily ever after in the kingdom, that's not true. The order to destroy the Jewish people still stands. Esther pours out her heart by falling at the king's feet, weeping and pleading mercy for her people. Her tears slowly stopped as she arises in response to the king's extended gold scepter.

Graciously and courageously Esther says, "If it pleases the king and if he regards me with favor and is pleased with me, let an order be written overruling the dispatches that Haman son of Hammedatha, the Agagite, devised and wrote to destroy the Jews in all the king's provinces. For how can I bear to see disaster fall on my people? How can I bear to see the destruction of my family?"

While Mordecai has come into an elevated position, only Esther can come to the king with so much passion about the planned destruction to come. The thought of these families being killed is unbearable as she begs for mercy. The counsel of his legal advisors is not needed. Again, as when he ruled on the death of Haman, we see the king take action for his queen's sake.

> ***The Esther reading group response:***
>
> ***She had the king's favor over everyone.***

The king gives the orders. Mordecai, in a new role, is now on the inside and in a position of great authority. The royal secretaries are given instructions about what to put in the new written decree, which is carried by couriers on fast horses especially bred for the king. It is like a major "e-news blast" sent to all 127 provinces from India to Cush.

He gives permission for the Jews to organize themselves for protection from anyone who tries to attack them. Mordecai leaves the king's presence with authority. Now, he wears the clothing of royalty—blue and white garments, a large crown of gold and a purple robe of fine linen.

God bestows on the Jews *a crown of beauty instead of ashes, the oil of gladness instead of mourning, and a garment of praise instead of a spirit of despair. They will be called oaks of righteousness, a planting of the Lord for the display of His splendor* (Isaiah 61:3). The people of other nationalities responded to all of this by becoming Jews themselves. It's a new season!

Do we allow non-believers to see how God is working in our lives to the point that they too become curious about knowing Him? Who wants to be on the Christian team? Those in the city of Susa were given a new lease on life because God intervened on behalf of His people. They sought God's help and He responded by helping them.

Haman is gone but his spirit lingered in his self-serving decree against the Jews. But, there is hope. They have permission to overpower those who come against them, and God will prevail against their enemies. God turns their situation around, and in this, there is a lesson for us.

The Jews were ready to face their enemies. They were united with a single purpose—to defeat their enemies. *The Jews assembled in their cities in all the provinces of King Xerxes to attack those seeking their destruction. They were an army led by God in His strength. No one could stand against them, because the people of all the other nationalities were afraid of them* (Esther 9:2).

Too often we do not assemble as a body when we are faced with spiritual attacks. We must recognize the devil's work and not allow him to have a foothold. The devil does not like the people of God to gather in the name of Jesus to read the Word, pray, worship, fellowship, conduct the affairs of the church and stand up for justice. The Bible teaches us not to be unaware of the devil's schemes; he comes to kill, steal and destroy.

Victory without unity is unlikely and the Jews knew it. Every province was organized for attack. They were so organized that their enemies became their allies in what they saw as a battle with an unfair advantage—God. Because of the alliance with the Jews, many were spared. Thousands were killed, including the ten sons of Haman.

Was It Worth It?

After the battle, Mordecai established an annual national celebration in memory of how God protected the Jews from their enemies. Their mourning became a time of celebration called Purim, which is still celebrated today.

Consider a Greater Purpose
Vashti, Esther and the Courageous Women who Followed

Mordecai became King Xerxes' second in command because he worked for the good of the people and refused to be silent concerning the welfare of all the Jews. This is truly a testimony of God's faithfulness and everlasting love. As Mordecai looked around at all God had done for him, Queen Esther and the Jews, he knew beyond a doubt that God took care of them during a great time of need.

Mordecai's elevation would not have happened without Esther's victory over Haman. God's mission was accomplished through the Queen, and the broader community played a key role. She came to the palace without knowing her destiny.

Similarly, Myrlie Evers-Williams, the widow of the late civil rights activist Medgar Evers, was instrumental in seeing that justice was brought to the man who cold-bloodedly murdered her husband. I had the pleasure of meeting her several years ago. She knew I was a clergy because we sat in the front rows of the auditorium in which she spoke for our Annual Celebration of the Life and Legacy of the Rev. Dr. Martin Luther King Jr.

I slowly approached Mrs. Evers-Williams at a table where she greeted and gave autographs. She is a beautiful courageous, woman of God. It's amazing how God uses others to give us just what we need at that very moment.

While she seems to be a pillar of the Civil Rights Movement, her rise into a leadership position was not one she sought. She married Medgar and together they had three children who they raised in Jackson, Mississippi. Although Medgar and other leaders of the National Association for the Advancement of

Accomplishing God's Mission

Colored People (NAACP) often had threats on their lives, they pursued efforts for voting rights, equal education and fair job opportunities.

On June 12, 1963, Medgar pulled into the family driveway; only he never made it into the house. He was killed by an assassin's bullet. He was just 37 years old. Immediately his wife became a widow, but his death would not be in vain. She would devote her life to seeking justice in the murder of her husband. That tragic event placed her in a position, "for such a time as this." Her boldness became one of strength seen by the African-American community that thrived on God, unity and the desire to be treated equally. She became a leader.

Trials to convict her husband's murderer were pointless. All-white juries of the South refused to convict one of their own in the killing of a Colored man who they felt was a threat to their way of life. Medgar had a history of wanting change for his people. He led boycotts against gas stations that denied Colored customers rights to the restrooms. He was a World War II Veteran and applied to the University of Mississippi School of Law, to no avail. He even led efforts for the investigation of the death of Chicago native, Emmett Till, a young teen killed after accusations that he spoke inappropriately to a White woman in the state of Mississippi. He was a radical in the eyes of southern racists.

For Myrlie, her children and African Americans, there seemed to be no justice in sight for her husband's murder. But Myrlie would not give up. Just as Queen Esther waited for the right time to approach the king to make her request, Myrlie prayed, waited and became an advocate for justice.

The wait paid off in 1989. She and her children had left the South, she was active in politics in California and she had remarried. Myrlie Evers-Williams still wanted justice in the death of Medgar. As years went on she learned of new evidence and witnesses who could testify that Byron De La Beckwith murdered her late husband. She pushed to have the case reopened and the evidence reexamined. She got more than she could imagine.

Those who heard the killer brag about what he had done testified against him. This time the jury wouldn't let him get away and in 1994, a jury of eight African Americans and four Whites, sentenced Beckwith to life in prison. He was 80 years old when he died in prison in 2001. Myrlie's tenacity and courage have inspired many today because she had victory, even if it was nearly forty years in the making. She finished her mission.

We witness Old Testament prophecy being fulfilled when God called a young woman by the name of Mary to be part of His plan of redemption to rescue humanity. God sent the angel Gabriel who approached Mary by saying, "Greetings, you who are highly favored! The Lord is with you."

These words sustained Mary. Later, she was overshadowed by the Holy Spirit and conceived the baby of promise. She carried God's son in her womb and had no sexual contact with Joseph during this time until after the consummation of their marriage.

Accomplishing God's Mission

After Jesus' birth the shepherds told her everything they knew concerning His life on earth. While everybody else was amazed, in Luke 2:19 it says, "But Mary treasured up all these things and pondered them in her heart." I imagine these words sustained her even at Jesus' crucifixion. She lived knowing He was sent to die for the sins of the world and to redeem His people. We cannot overlook the courage it took for Mary to glorify God all the way to the cross where the Son of God was crucified.

About two years in the pastorate of Immanuel Christian Reformed Church, I had the privilege of joining a delegation on a trip to New York City. That trip included a meeting with the first African-American evangelist and ordained minister in our denomination, the Rev. Dr. Eugene Callendar.

In the 1950's, he reached many lost souls, helped start a drug addiction treatment center, dealt with landlords who charged tenants too much rent, and built a strong inner-city outreach ministry in Harlem. He helped extend the reach of Christian Reformed Home Missions and the *Back to God Hour's* Christian radio ministry into the African-American community.

The same year we met, he planned to come to Kalamazoo, Michigan, to the Fetzer Center. I couldn't resist inviting him to be our guest preacher the Sunday he was in town. He accepted our invitation. He expressed to me how proud he was that I was called to pastor a Christian Reformed church. The city newspaper, the *Kalamazoo Gazette* contacted me about writing a feature on Callendar. Their interest, was on the fact that in 1959, he had been asked to leave the Christian Reformed denomination after his divorce. He had not returned to speak in our denomination until this visit to Kalamazoo.

Consider a Greater Purpose
Vashti, Esther and the Courageous Women who Followed

Some didn't understand why I wanted him to speak. But, I needed him to come back to a place where his story encouraged and inspired so many. For me, he was a trailblazer! The story, *A Blessing in Disguise,* highlighted Dr. Callendar's visit to speak for the first time in the denomination that exiled him.

Callendar acknowledged bitter feelings at the time of his departure from the denomination. He had long since realized his departure from the CRC was a blessing in disguise. He said the move allowed him to branch out in his work, giving him the chance to eventually become pastor of the largest Presbyterian church in New York City and to serve as an advisor to five U.S. presidents.

When I first met Dr. Callendar, I asked, "Was it worth it?" As he looked back over his life and career, I wanted to know if being in it was a meaningful experience. He understood what I meant. We had something in common. At the time, I was one of only two African-American female pastors in the CRC and served in an inner-city church.

"Yes," he answered. After he came to Kalamazoo and preached at Immanuel Church, I asked again, "Was it worth it?" He answered, "Yes, but it wasn't easy." He went on to say how it was "a springboard that allowed him to take his ministry in new directions and to give his social justice ministry a much larger scope." He was fulfilling God's call. Those words have stayed with me. When I wanted to quit, those words sustained me for the path marked out for me by God. I think if asked, Mrs. Myrlie Evers-Williams and Mary, the mother of Jesus, would say it wasn't easy…but it was worth it.

Accomplishing God's Mission

As *The Banner Magazine* stated, "Posie is herself a trailblazer as one of the first African-American women to pastor a Christian Reformed Church, and her ministry also focuses on racial and social outreach." The Rev. Peter Borgdorff, Executive Director of Ministries for the CRC, at that time was quoted, "Callendar helped to begin the kind of urban ministry in the CRC that Posie is now doing in Kalamazoo."

I am one among many women who have been used by God "for such a time as this" at various times in our journey. The reality of this became clear after discovering how often I have had the privilege to hold positions not typically held by women and/or an African American. I was the first African American woman resident assistant of a graduate dorm at Columbia International University. God led me to pastor Immanuel, where I was the first African American and first woman pastor. While in Kalamazoo I was appointed the first woman vice president of the Northside Ministerial Alliance and elected the first woman president shortly thereafter.

All things in life are purposeful. God opened the door for me to serve men, women, boys and girls in churches, schools, prisons, jails, seminaries, the streets, with individuals, families, small groups, organizations and congregations. Each one of these positions came with its unique risks and challenges. However, nothing was more evident to me than God's call, strength, love and anointing for each mission. Although it wasn't easy, it was worth it.

Consider a Greater Purpose
Vashti, Esther and the Courageous Women who Followed

Esther

An ordinary young woman used mightily by God. Accepts her childhood misfortunes. Maintains loyalty to Mordecai. Surrenders to God's will in a time of uncertainty. Walks in God's favor. Becomes the new queen. Assesses the situation facing her people. Knows the Persian laws. Uses her position to help others. Surrounds herself with the support of others. Shows wisdom in approaching the challenge. Depends on God's mercy. Acts decisively. Stands up for the injustices against her people. Blesses Mordecai. And saves her people.

Accomplishing God's Mission

Reflections

1. What concern does "being outside of the king's gate" present for you? What example in life illustrates what this means to you?

2. How has a tragic event in your life been a blessing in disguise?

3. What are five characteristics others mention to you as standing out in regard to how you serve others?

4. When have you had to plead on behalf of someone else? What was the outcome? Why was it worth it? Why were you drawn to be involved?

5. What aspects of this biblical story are similar to your story of how God uses ordinary "you" to accomplish His mission?

Prayer
Father, it is my desire to be obedient to Your will. I will stay in the race until I reach the finish line. You will carry me all the way until my assignment is done. May You receive all the honor and glory for every opportunity You give me to make a difference for the advancement of Your kingdom. May people be blessed as You work through my life to accomplish Your will. You will give me the wisdom, faith and endurance to run this race. In Jesus name.
AMEN.

Notes

# A Letter from Esther to 21ˢᵗ Century Women of Courage

A Letter from Esther

Dear Women of God in 21st Century America,

And who knows but that you have come to royal position for such a time as this? Let your greatest desire be to please the King. I was nobody, powerless and a Jew. I was an outsider. That didn't matter to God. I really want you to hear my voice and see my perspective.

Of the many books written about the book of Esther, I don't think much attention is given to how God used a woman like me to deliver His people. I am a real person, not a figure of imagination created by someone. God created a real woman. Don't waste valuable time trying to be somebody without realizing that only God molds and shapes those He uses for His purposes. When we try to find significance in life, without God, it is useless. You have to release yourself to Him. He knows the plans for you.

Mordecai said to me, "…And who knows?" God knew what purpose He had in mind for my life. That's all that matters. You will never reach your potential in life unless you follow where He leads. Are you learning to recognize His hand? It requires times being alone before Him away from the busyness of work, family, friends and even ministry. Sometimes He allows us to be in a situation whereas there is no one else to lean on but Him. That is what happened to me. Maybe you can relate.

My safety net, Mordecai, was gone when I entered the gates of the palace. All of us have a safety net or two; what are yours? Who or what are you relying on more than God? Sometimes we become so attached to our careers, material possessions, status, giftedness—and, yes, even our ministries and churches that we don't know what God has put inside of us. If any of these things are taken away, where will it leave you? Would you be able to trust God anyhow? Would you lose your rhythm in life?

Would you be so off track that you are paralyzed? Maybe you are like me. I did not realize how much I relied on Mordecai until God brought me to a new place, a place I had never been before. He thought just maybe I became too comfortable in my royal position. Mordecai didn't realize that in his absence, God had been growing me up. I was no longer his little girl.

If he had known this, he would not have spoken so strongly about my being in the king's house as if that was all I had going for me. By the time I learned of the bad news concerning my people, I was at a point in life where God was all I had. I was thoroughly committed to doing His will because He brought me through a process of surrender. I was confident that God would take care of the results.

Now, when I look back, I see nothing but God's favor. I experienced His favor in the past, but never to this extent. It seemed like He kept opening doors that I just walked through without manipulation, fight or plea to gain the king's approval. King Xerxes' focus was on finding a queen; God's focus was on making a servant. I am a servant of God. Through my life, He saved His people.

When He makes a servant, He uses her. Many of us want to be used by God but we are not worshippers. We worship Him for who He is. If he does nothing or nothing else, His name should be exalted. True worship leads us into surrender. We let go. Obedience becomes a strong desire. Behavior aligns with His will. We live in such a way that every now and then we

A Letter from Esther

sense God is smiling on us! The more we know Him, the more we want to please Him. Giving ourselves to Him comes after He reveals Himself to us. Then we are open to be stretched by Him in service. He gives the opportunities; we don't have to look for them. He will lead us.

You have many distractions today. It's easy to put your trust in something or someone other than God. I trusted Him even when I was forced to go to the palace. I trusted from day one, but still while I was there my faith was enlarged so that my feet would not slip. When it came time for the greater assignment, I was ready. God makes you ready. I stopped thinking about those things that bring people happiness; God helped me to see those things that are important to Him. I considered a greater purpose.

I did not blindly come into my marriage relationship. No, Hegai taught me things about the king. Many women get married today without even learning what marriage is about. It was different for me; Hegai taught me how to be a queen. Who's teaching you how to be a queen? Concubines and queens don't behave the same way. The standards are higher for queens. Know the difference and chose to live as a queen!

The longer I was with my mentor, the more I got to know the king. Who knew the king better than Hegai? I was motivated to know him because I wanted to please him as his wife not as a concubine. Too many young ladies are settling for the concubine role instead of preparing to be a wife. The benefits in being a wife are far greater than being a concubine. Don't settle for less!

Consider a Greater Purpose
Vashti, Esther and the Courageous Women who Followed

Even in our spiritual life, we settle for the, I'll-be-with-You-When-I-Need-You fellowship with our Heavenly Father rather than a constant fellowship with Him. It all begins with a desire. The Apostle Paul passionately and consistently prayed for the Ephesians, "the glorious Father, may give you the Spirit of wisdom and revelation, so that you may know him better" (Ephesians 1:17).

Knowing God is powerful and profitable. I am not talking about knowing about Him, but knowing Him. Let your desire be to deeply love Him. I never let my royal position keep me from growing intimately with God. This is what it takes for Him to walk closely with us. Have you allowed a new position, relationship or activity to keep you from growing intimately with God?

When Mordecai said, "but that you have come to royal position..." in that moment I knew God brought me here "for such a time as this." I began to think about all that had happened to me from the day I was brought to the palace. God will never have us do something where He does not provide the provisions. It was no mistake that I had been exalted to a royal position to help God's people. I believed it was by His providence that I was in a position to serve a doomed people. I was chosen to serve the king as his wife, but there was a greater purpose – to serve God. I was the right person, in the right place and at the right time. I believed that justice would prevail. I knew this deep inside.

It is easy to be blindsided by the ordinary without seeing how God wants to use you for an extraordinary work. This was a divine assignment and I knew it from the bottom of my heart. My deepest desire above all things, even my own desires, passions and needs, is to serve the Lord. His fingerprints were everywhere in my life. Mordecai knew it, but he thought I got caught up in the king and all the royalty. You can imagine getting caught up in a five or six-figure salary with amenities. God has always been near to Mordecai. But what he didn't know was that I continued to grow in my relationship with God.

In fact, I got to know God better in the palace than when I was living in the province. Location makes no difference to God; it is never a barrier. He's everywhere and we are not out of His reach! What do you believe about His providence concerning where you are in life? What circumstances did He use to bring you to where you are in life? Are you growing in your faith right where you are?

"For such a time as this" relates to a specific time. I learned that my people needed to be rescued and I was in a position to help them. Could I have ignored it? It was all in God's timing. It was not a "just so happen" thing. He needed me in this very moment. If you are walking in obedience and sometimes even disobedience with God, He might show you where He needs you to serve for the good of others.

Abraham walked in obedience; Jonah walked in disobedience for a while. My people needed to be rescued. I saw God's fingerprints on the situation and it made it easier for me to respond, "Yes, Lord!" I had a stronger conviction after our time of fasting and prayer.

You should consider doing a timeline of your life or a map of seasons in your life listing significant events or benchmarks to see how God led you to where you are right now. Don't be like some women who never stop to exhale to see what God is teaching them. Don't miss out on anything He wants to give. God requires our attention in all situations. He desires us to look to Him at all times. Pray, pray and pray.

There is a price to pay in being at one with God. I was willing to pay the price of being thrown out of the palace or even losing my own life to fulfill His purpose. I meant it when I said, "And if I perish, I perish." When I spoke these words, in my heart, I knew I was sold out to God. I love Him with all my heart, mind, soul and strength. There are those who say they will follow and there are also those who actually follow God; there is a difference. If I tried to do this on my own, I would have messed up everything. He was there for me and I knew it. He gave me what to say and when to say it.

Don't think God is not strategic. He was asking me to get involved with saving His people. Doesn't this sound like a big request? He was letting me know that there is nothing too big or complicated for Him. Sometimes God asks us to do big things for Him to affect the lives of others. Is He speaking now?

My response is a powerful testimony of my love for our God. I could not have done any of this without my faith in Him. My obedience in responding to His will is motivated by my love. Does that make sense to you? Even if I disobeyed God, like Mordecai said, "relief and deliverance for the Jews will arise from another place, but (me) and (my) family will perish." To me those were some strong and unnecessary words. Mordecai just didn't understand where I stood concerning my obedience to God.

A Letter from Esther

Oftentimes people on the outside make wrong assumptions about you. That's what he did about me. Since I have been in the palace, God taught me how to stand firm believing in His word and strength, coupled with prayer. It didn't take any persuasion to ask the Jews to pray and fast for me. I needed God's strength, and I knew they were willing to sacrifice. I desired above all things to obey God. This assignment was entrusted to me and I took it seriously. There was no hesitation on my part. It's not difficult to obey when you've experienced His faithful love.

How does your testimony reflect His faithful love for you? In what ways are your actions motivated by His faithful love? I hope the sermons you listen to and the Bible studies you attend are balanced. What I mean is that too much about "you" and too little about God isn't good. I've learned about who I am through knowing Him. In fact, I believe it is the only way to know your "true self." I recognize His character and nature in me because He has revealed himself to me, through His grace. No one is perfect, but my deepest desire in life was to know God. It paid off!

God uses women to change the world in powerful ways even when the odds are against us. I am the face of many women desiring to be used by Him to make a difference in the world. More women like me are in the Body of Christ.

The 21st Century needs women of God who speak truth about the failure of systems and structures that harm and even destroy people. You cannot become too comfortable and forget about those who need your leadership. How hot is your fire for a worthy cause? Who keeps coming to mind as someone needing an advocate? In what ways is God making you ready for a royal position? How responsive are you?

Consider a Greater Purpose
Vashti, Esther and the Courageous Women who Followed

You have so many wonderful role models from the past and present to glean from. Some of them appear in this book, but there are many more. Continue to learn from them. Spend time with those women who walk the talk. Pray for them. Emulate them. Give and be willing to receive. God gives so that you have something to give to others. Sow seeds for a harvest of righteous.

Remember, my obedience to God reflects the obedience of His own Son, Jesus Christ. I did nothing out of selfish ambition but obeyed God for a greater purpose.

"Each of you should look not only to your own interests, but also to the interests of others" (Philippians 2:4). "Your attitude should be the same as that of Christ Jesus: Who, being in very nature God, did not consider equality with God something to be grasped, but made Himself nothing, taking the very nature of a servant, being made in human likeness. And being found in appearance as a man, He humbled Himself and became obedient to death – even death on a cross" (Philippians 2:5-8).

He made himself nothing by not allowing others to make Him their earthly king because they wanted deliverance from the hands of the Romans. He did not ask the Father to save Him from going to the cross. He knew it was why He came. Obedience is motivated by love. There is no greater love! This truth is revealed in Jesus words, "I will not speak with you much longer (speaking to his disciples), for the prince of this world is coming. He has no hold on me, but the world must learn that I love the Father and that I do exactly what My Father has commanded Me" (John 14:30-31).

A Letter from Esther

Jesus told the Pharisees, "I tell you the truth, the Son can do nothing by Himself; He can do only what He sees His Father doing, because whatever the Father does the Son also does. For the Father loves the Son and shows Him all He does. Yes, to your amazement He will show Him even greater things than these" (John 5:19-20).

God shows you what to do in life—in good and bad times. You have to know Him for yourself. Haman had no hold on me; God did. Mordecai's initial reaction was fear, but once I sent word back by Hathach, he was at ease. He understood that God had chosen me as a vessel to save His people. I am so thankful to Him for using me. Nothing means more to me in life.

He has chosen all of you for something that will benefit others far greater than you can imagine. People need to taste and see that He is good. People need to hear about what He has taught you so that they can experience true freedom from whatever keeps them from surrendering to His will. They might need to hear that He came to earth as a living, holy sacrifice for sinful man.

Such a great cloud of witnesses surrounds you. I am one of them. Consider the need for social justice today. The woman called for such a time as this is open to God's leading to positions of influence, power and where He needs her to make a great impact for kingdom gain. She knows how to walk alone. She does not allow promotions to keep her from doing her Father's business. She understands that it is not about her, but "The Lord works righteousness and justice for all the oppressed" (Psalm 103:6). She has this purpose in mind. She looks beyond where she is currently to see her role in paving the way for the next generation. She understands that systems are failing: education, law and justice, and the family institution. She is concerned with issues like the young dying to violence, premarital sexual relationships, the rise in domestic violence and many other social ills.

So many women of all races, ages and backgrounds have been encouraged by how God used me for a great purpose. They say I was pretty and smart, powerful and strategically positioned to be abundantly blessed. Some say, I was positioned for greatness. This was God's doing; He gave me favor, which I did not deserve. I, even, love my man. I am grateful for everything! I would sometimes be overwhelmed that God used me for such a time as this!

As you encounter girls and women who want to know about our loving and awesome God, tell them about Vashti, me and the courageous women who followed. Pray for their hearts to be open to the things of God. Teach them to emulate us and those women who are living transformed lives. We considered a greater purpose.

To God be the glory!

Reflections

1. Respond to Esther's letter. What thoughts come to mind?

2. What questions or concerns do you have about being used by God for his purposes? Is anything or anyone holding you back?

3. How has God called you "for such a time as time?" What is your response?

4. Who are some of those "great cloud of witnesses" surrounding you?

5. Consider writing your own story of courage. What might be the title?

Prayer

Lord, I yearn to live in the greater purposes of God. If anything is holding me back from experiencing the fullness of your love and grace, please set me free from all hindrances. You are my King, Redeemer and Lord of Lords! There is none like you. I desire your will for my life. I'm open to the guidance of your Holy Spirit leading me in the path of righteousness. Help me desire to live beyond mere lip service and to be sensitive to other women who live in the greater purposes of God. Help me to understand, encourage and help them. Help me to tell my own story and to be a witness to others of your greatness, faithfulness and love. In your mighty name I pray. AMEN.

Afterword

Afterword

I wanted to share my thoughts on the book of Esther and make it available to women desiring to be used by God beyond what they could ask or imagine. To me, "for such a time as this" conveys something out of the ordinary. This statement is applicable for women who are living in the great purposes of God.

When I was younger I thought I had to figure everything out for myself and for my life. It was not until I experienced God in the valley, wilderness and fire that I began to learn obedience. For me, there is no better place and time to know God. He knows how to get our full attention. Strangely, these can be some of the most powerful and fruit bearing times. This kind of preparation is also one of the mysteries of being positioned for a greater purpose.

As I look back, one of my greatest discoveries was that God prepared me each time for my next assignment. I could not fill in the blanks about what I was going to do or where I was going. All I knew is that there was an inner yearning to follow the Holy Spirit and trust him to lead me to places, positions and people. It was not based on my personal preference. We are who we are because of the people whom God uses to influence and even challenge our thinking and behavior.

In preparation for writing this book God positioned women around me who had experienced racism, sexism, abuse, the murder of a child, and other worldly suffering and pain. These women were participants in the Esther reading group that helped in the creation of this book. As we read the book of Esther, there was a lot of energy, laughter and interactions.

Afterword

What was so great is that they were told at the beginning to introduce themselves but not to reveal their profession. Each person made a more formal introduction at the very end.

An owner of a thriving magazine, authors, Ph.D.'s, teachers, a hair stylist, program directors, the retired, students, a police official, administrators, a mom who home schools her two children, and some pastors were participants. It is not unusual that some of them work in fields dominated by men and they are the first women to hold a particular position.

Many of them are still talking about this event and want more like it. I am very pleased that they received the invitation with an openness to receive from God—and He poured into us! They were encouraged to continue praying and thinking about what God would continue to teach them through Esther. Their thoughts stimulated the writing process for me. Many of their comments were used throughout this book. I decided to use this form of engagement after talking to Dr. Carol Bechtel, who wrote an interpretation of the book of Esther. I suggest that you try something similar. I took some liberties in using my "sanctified imagination" in writing this book, but the story of Esther is preserved.

I appreciate and honor women of all ethnicities, ages, socioeconomic backgrounds, educational levels, and faiths who are trailblazers—past, present and future—who are willing to "rock the boat." I desire to leave a legacy for the next generations and I pray you do as well. Remember, God uses the most unlikely individuals and seemingly insignificant places to impact the world.

Afterword

If I had the opportunity to ask Mary, Mother of Jesus, "Was it worth it?" I believe she would say, "Yes, but it wasn't easy." *For God so loved the world that he gave His one and only Son, that whoever believes in Him shall not perish but have eternal life. For God did not send His Son into the world to condemn the world, but to save the world through Him (John 3:16-17).*

If I had the opportunity to ask Esther, "Was it worth it?" I believe she would say, "Yes, but it wasn't easy." Some thought she was just another pretty face vying for a place in the kingdom. Maybe even Esther thought she was just another face in the crowd. But God used her mightily to save the Jews. As queen, she had everything! As a yielded vessel, she was willing to give it all up, even her life, to save her people. We do not know if the selection of Esther as queen was a unanimous one by all who participated in the search process. But, it really didn't matter. God elevates for His purposes!

The Author

The Author

Denise L. Posie was ordained in 1999, at Tabernacle Missionary Baptist Church in Detroit, Michigan, under the leadership of the late Rev. Dr. Frederick G. Sampson. She currently serves as pastor-congregation consultant in the Christian Reformed Church in North America in the Office of Pastor-Church Relations in Grand Rapids, Michigan. Prior to this current assignment she served for thirteen years as pastor of Immanuel Christian Reformed Church in Kalamazoo, Michigan.

She has an Associate of Arts degree in General Studies from Wayne County Community College, a Bachelor of Arts degree in Business Administration from Marygrove College, (both in Detroit), and a Master of Divinity degree in Pastoral Leadership from Columbia International University in Columbia, South Carolina (1999).

Posie has spoken at conferences and workshops and has facilitated leadership retreats in addition to preaching in pulpits. She has published in *Reformed Worship,* "Black and Reformed: Perspective from Five African American Leaders" March 2006; and *Weavings Journal,* "Rising with New Courage and New Hope" Volume XXIV, Number 2, March/April 2009, an issue dedicated to the teachings of Parker J. Palmer.

She currently resides in West Michigan where she enjoys friendships, reading, journaling and encouraging the young and mature to know their God-given gifts. In addition, she is a featured speaker at various venues throughout the country.

The Author

Denise L. Posie founded DLP Ministries (Daily Living with Purpose) in 2012 as a way to join God in advancing the kingdom through preaching, teaching, training and conversations that equip and challenge individuals to grow in Christ. She envisions transformed lives, honoring and glorifying God.

To contact Denise L. Posie write to:

DLP Ministries
P.O. Box 117
Kalamazoo, MI 49004-0117

or e-mail:
dlpministries7@gmail.com

Bibliography & Further Reading

Achtemeier, Paul J. Harper's Bible Dictionary (Harper & Row, Society of Biblical Literature, 1985)

Angelou, Maya. *I Know Why The Caged Bird Sings* (New York, Random House, 1970)

Atkinson, Morgan C. with Montaldo, Jonathan ed. *Soul Searching*. The Journey of Thomas Merton (Collegeville, Minnesota, Liturgical Press, 2008)

Bechtel, Carol M. *Esther*. Interpretation, A Bible Commentary for Teaching and Preaching (Louisville, John Knox Press, 2002)

Brand, Chad, Draper, Charles, England, Archie (Gen. Eds.) Holman Illustrated Bible Dictionary (Nashville, TN, Holman Bible Publishers, 2003)

Breneman, Mervin. *Ezra, Nehemiah, Esther*. The New American Commentary, v. 10 (Nashville, Broadman & Holman Publishers, 1993)

Dell, Pamela. *Wilma Mankiller*. Chief of the Cherokee Nation (Minneapolis, Compass Point Books. 2006)

Felix, Antonia. *Sonia Sotomayor*. The True American Dream (New York, The Berkley Publishing Group, 2010)

Fluker, Walter & Tumber, Catherine (Eds.) *A Strange Freedom*. The Best of Howard Thurman on Religious Experience and Public Life (Boston, Beacon Press, 1998)

Gerber, Robin. *Leadership the Eleanor Roosevelt Way* (New York, Press Hall Press, 2002)

Height, Dorothy. *Open Wide the Freedom Gates* (New York, Public Affairs, a member of the Perseus Books Group, 2003)

Hine, Darlene Clark, Brown, Elsa Barkley, Terborg-Penn, Rosalyn ed. *Black Women in America.* An Historical Encyclopedia, v. II (Bloomington & Indianapolis, Indiana University Press, 1993)

Kolodiejchuk, Brian M.C. *Mother TERESA,* Come Be My Light (New York, Doubleday, 2007)

Lewis, C. S. *Mere Christianity* (New York, Harper Collins Publishers, 1952)

Ling, Chai. *A Heart for Freedom* (Carol Stream, IL, Tyndale House Publishers, Inc., 2011)

Mankiller, Wilma. *Mankiller,* A Chief and Her People (New York, St. Martin's Press, 1993)

Myers, Allen C. (Rev. Ed.) Eerdmans Bible Dictionary, (Grand Rapids, MI, William B. Eerdmans Publishing Company, 1987)

Roberts, Robin. *From the Heart.* Seven Rules to Live By (New York, Hyperion, 2007)

The Banner, CRC's First Black Pastor Returns 42 Years After Bitter Farewell, May 21, 2001 written by Chris Meehan.